THE HISTORY OF BIROBIDZHAN

Russian Shorts
Russian Shorts is a series of thought-provoking books published in a slim format. The Shorts books examine key concepts, personalities, and moments in Russian historical and cultural studies, encompassing its vast diversity from the origins of the Kievan state to Putin's Russia. Each book is intended for a broad range of readers, covers a side of Russian history and culture that has not been well-understood, and is meant to stimulate conversation.

Series Editors:
Eugene M. Avrutin, Professor of Modern European Jewish History, University of Illinois, USA
Stephen M. Norris, Professor of History, Miami University, USA

Editorial Board:
Edyta Bojanowska, Professor of Slavic Languages and Literatures, Yale University, USA
Ekaterina Boltunova, Associate Professor of History, Higher School of Economics, Russia
Eliot Borenstein, Professor of Russian and Slavic, New York University, USA
Melissa Caldwell, Professor of Anthropology, University of California Santa Cruz, USA
Choi Chatterjee, Professor of History, California State University, Los Angeles, USA
Robert Crews, Professor of History, Stanford University, USA
Dan Healey, Professor of Modern Russian History, University of Oxford, UK
Polly Jones, Associate Professor of Russian, University of Oxford, UK
Paul R. Josephson, Professor of History, Colby College, USA
Marlene Laruelle, Research Professor of International Affairs, George Washington University, USA
Marina Mogilner, Associate Professor, University of Illinois at Chicago, USA
Willard Sunderland, Henry R. Winkler Professor of Modern History, University of Cincinnati, USA

Published Titles
Pussy Riot: Speaking Punk to Power, Eliot Borenstein
Memory Politics and the Russian Civil War: Reds Versus Whites, Marlene Laruelle and Margarita Karnysheva
Russian Utopia: A Century of Revolutionary Possibilities, Mark Steinberg
Racism in Modern Russia, Eugene M. Avrutin
Meanwhile, In Russia: Russian Memes and Viral Video Culture, Eliot Borenstein

THE HISTORY OF BIROBIDZHAN

BUILDING A SOVIET JEWISH HOMELAND IN SIBERIA

Gennady Estraikh

BLOOMSBURY ACADEMIC

LONDON • NEW YORK • OXFORD • NEW DELHI • SYDNEY

BLOOMSBURY ACADEMIC
Bloomsbury Publishing Plc
50 Bedford Square, London, WC1B 3DP, UK
1385 Broadway, New York, NY 10018, USA
29 Earlsfort Terrace, Dublin 2, Ireland

BLOOMSBURY, BLOOMSBURY ACADEMIC and the Diana logo are
trademarks of Bloomsbury Publishing Plc

First published in Great Britain 2023

Cover image: Russia (© Yarr65/Alamy Stock Photo).

Series design by Tjaša Krivec

Bloomsbury Publishing Plc does not have any control over, or responsibility
for, any third-party websites referred to or in this book. All internet addresses
given in this book were correct at the time of going to press. The author and
publisher regret any inconvenience caused if addresses have changed or sites
have ceased to exist, but can accept no responsibility for any such changes.

Every effort has been made to trace the copyright holders and obtain
permission to reproduce the copyright material. Please do get in touch with
any enquiries or any information relating to such material or the rights holder.
We would be pleased to rectify any omissions in subsequent editions of this
publication should they be drawn to our attention.

A catalogue record for this book is available from the British Library.

A catalog record for this book is available from the Library of Congress.

ISBN: PB: 978-1-3502-9624-4
         HB: 978-1-3502-9623-7
         ePDF: 978-1-3502-9625-1
         eBook: 978-1-3502-9626-8

Typeset by RefineCatch, Bungay, Suffolk
Printed and bound in Great Britain

To find out more about our authors and books visit www.bloomsbury.com
and sign up for our newsletters.

CONTENTS

FIGURES

ABBREVIATIONS

Agro-Joint	American Jewish Joint Agricultural Corporation
Ambijan	American Committee for the Settlement of Jews in Birobidjan
JAR	Jewish Autonomous Region
JDC	American Jewish Joint Distribution Committee
ICOR	Organization for Jewish Colonization in Russia
KOMZET	Committee for the Settlement of Toiling Jews on the Land
NEP	New Economic Policy
NKVD	People's Commissariat for Internal Affairs
ORT	Organization for the Distribution of Artisanal and Agricultural Skills among the Jews (since 1921 World ORT Union, or Organization for Rehabilitation through Traning)
OZET	Association for the Settlement of Toiling Jews on the Land

ACKNOWLEDGMENTS

I had a chance to be born in Birobidzhan, the administrative center of the Jewish Autonomous Region (JAR) in the Far East of Russia. Before 1941, when my father was drafted to serve in World War II and my mother and older siblings were evacuated to Central Asia, they lived in a Jewish village in Ukraine, which was established around 1850 and ceased being Jewish under the Nazi occupation. After the war, my parents were thinking about moving to Birobidzhan, especially as Yiddish was the language of their upbringing and education. Ultimately, they changed their mind and settled in a Ukrainian city.

The word "Birobidzhan" probably entered my lexicon around 1960, when my parents took me to see the newly released 1936 movie *Seekers of Happiness*, a propaganda piece about foreign settlers coming to the JAR. In the 1970s, we subscribed to *Birobidzhaner Shtern* (Birobidzhan Star) and in the mid-1980s this Yiddish newspaper published my first journalistic attempts in Yiddish. Birobidzhan was regularly mentioned and described in the Moscow Yiddish literary monthly *Sovetish Heymland* (Soviet Homeland), which employed me as the managing editor in 1988–91, the last years of the Soviet era. The journal's editor-in-chief, Aron Vergelis, and associate editor, Chaim Beider, had Birobidzhan periods in their lives. My academic interests, heavily focused on Jewish life under communism, drew me to various aspects of the Birobidzhan history and, finally, brought me to writing this book.

I would like to thank my colleagues who helped me during my work on this book: Iosif Brener, Ber Boris Kotlerman, Alexander Frenkel, Alexander Ivanov, Elena Sarashevskaia and Valery Gurevich. Special thanks to Eugene Avrutin and Stephen Norris who encouraged me and pointed to weaknesses in the draft of the manuscript. Thanks also to Sandra Creaser for her meticulous editorial attention to the text.

INTRODUCTION

The Bolsheviks, or Communists as they began calling themselves in 1918, envisioned a radical plan for the world: to tear entirely the existing social and economic fabric and to build instead a new civilization. This was how the future looked to the Vladimir Lenin-led revolutionary cohort, and their dream had found a reflection in the lyrics of their anthem, the Russian version of "The Internationale": "We will destroy the whole world of violence/To the bottom and then/ We are ours, we will build a new world...." Chaim Gildin, a Soviet Yiddish writer, poeticized in the 1920s: "Lenin enjoined me— / to lead the old world, like a dog on a leash, to its grave."[1]

It was easier to dream and sing than to act. In reality, the Soviet regime, established by the Bolsheviks in 1917, inherited numerous peculiarities and problems of Imperial Russia, including the so-called "Jewish question." The Russian emperors, or tsars, and their governments tried to find a solution to it from the end of the 18th century, after annexing vast areas in what used to be the Polish-Lithuanian Commonwealth. A nation that historically had not tolerated Jews, saw itself suddenly confronted with large agglomerations of Yiddish-speaking followers of Judaism, inextricably entwined in the economy as a vital part of its merchant and artisan component. The annexed territories, punctuated with heavily Jewish *shtetls*, or market towns, formed in the Russian Empire the core of an area legally delineated as the Pale of Jewish Settlement.

Marginally and incrementally successful attempts were made to homogenize the Jews, particularly through education, military service and agricultural colonization. Conversion to Christianity was welcomed but constituted a relatively minor phenomenon. Although several social and professional groups of the Jewish population— mainly wealthy merchants and entrepreneurs, university graduates, skillful artisans, and some army veterans—were gradually allowed to settle outside the Pale, full emancipation came only after the fall of the empire in 1917.

By the end of the 19th century, Russian Jewry had grown to over five million, constituting four percent of the total population of the empire. Ninety-four percent of them lived within the boundaries of the Pale and the Russian-controlled Kingdom of Poland, where different rules and regulations governed Jews. To a great degree, the Jews remained a parallel society, separated legally, religiously, socially, linguistically and even gastronomically. Although abject poverty and social depravity were widespread, it would be an exaggeration to generalize about the Jews as the most disadvantaged group of the empire's population. Many thousands had been well integrated into the economy of the country and its professional community. A tiny minority belonged to the aristocracy or other highly privileged strata of society. Jews were conspicuous among the *intelligentsia*, a social stratum of educated people committed to using their cultural capital to the benefit of society. A network of Jewish religious, philanthropic, cultural and financial organizations operated legally (albeit with restrictions) at the local and national level. Significantly, Russian Jews had considerably longer life expectancy than ethnic Russians.[2]

An increasing number of Russian Jews stood with one leg in traditional society and with the other in the non-Jewish world. The social space, sandwiched between Jewish and Christian societies and distinct in its lifestyle, organization, values and behavior, provided an important recruiting ground for diverse political and cultural movements and groupings. Meanwhile, economic underdevelopment, residence and occupational restrictions, outbreaks of violence (pogroms), political repression and ill treatment in the army pushed hundreds of thousands of Jews to emigrate, predominantly to the United States, where they formed communities deeply concerned with what was happening in the "old country."

The revolution brought profound changes to the status and living conditions of the Jews. Under the Soviet government, they enjoyed full equality before the law, but continued to experience severe strains exacerbated by fallouts from the world and civil wars on the one hand and by the post-revolutionary social and economic transformations on the other. The pre-revolutionary Bolsheviks' program regarding the Jews was paltry at best, but after coming to power they faced the task of dealing with this segment of the population. Hence, the institutional framework of the new regime included the Commissariat for Jewish Affairs and the Jewish Sections in the Communist Party. Neither the Commissariat in the government of Soviet Russia nor the Jewish Sections became Moscow-based central bodies for the entire Soviet Union, or in its full name the Union of Soviet Socialist Republics (USSR), formed in December 1922 as a federation of ethnic republics stretched over most of the erstwhile imperial territories. Rather, similar structures appeared also in the Ukrainian and Belorussian republics. The vast majority of Soviet Jews lived in the three Slavic republics, with the highest share, 61 percent, in Ukraine, then in Russia, 21 percent, and Belorussia, now Belarus, 16 percent (the figures are for 1926).

The Commissariat (1918–1924) and the Jewish Sections (1918–1930) were instrumental, first, in engaging and ideologically straightening out apostates from various Jewish political groupings and, second, in liquidating or placing under the state's control the intricate network of Jewish organizations built before and in the early years after the revolution. The coveted and ultimately achieved result aimed at turning the Jews into a state-controlled, increasingly secularized segment of the general population. Meanwhile, the Commissariat and the Jewish Sections did little for addressing the economic woes that had been haunting the Jews. In 1926, Shimen (Semen) Dimanshtein, a Lubavitch yeshiva graduate turned Bolshevik and a top functionary responsible for Jewish issues, summarized the situation by admitting that the revolution had brought misfortune to the majority of Jews.[3]

Dimanshtein did not mean the growing Jewish membership in the Communist Party, the rapidly expanding Jewish student body, and the professionally qualified and otherwise employable Jews who had procured positions at all levels of the bureaucracy, industry, retail, education, culture, academia, army and police. Rather, he pointed at the self-employed artisans, individual petty traders, former business and property owners, and religious functionaries unable to find a steady place in the emerging Soviet mainstream. In addition to those who fell on hard times after the revolution, the shtetl always had the so-called *luftmentschn*, "people suspended in mid-air," unable to fend for themselves. The idea of transforming the amorphous and "worthless" underclass—Jewish petty and déclassé bourgeois as well as *luftmentschn*—into toiling workers and peasants gripped the imagination of Soviet leaders in the early 1920s.

The government took particular interest in Jewish farming, seeing it as an effective way of providing at least some economically deprived shtetl dwellers with a useful and self-sufficient way of life. Especially as hundreds of shtetl Jews had turned to peri-urban agriculture by their own initiative, in an effort to survive in the new economic environment. Small groups of Zionist youth also had established several kibbutz-like settlements as training grounds for future life in Palestine. After the state took matters into its own hands, the scale of the endeavor considerably increased: tens of thousands of Jews got encouraged to engage in agricultural activities, mainly in the Ukrainian and Belorussian republics as well as in Crimea, then part of the Russian Republic.

Becoming a peasant was also a way to upgrade the social standing of a person categorized as *lishenets*, or "disenfranchised." In addition to being deprived of their voting rights, families carrying the stigma of belonging to this category were discriminated against in access to education, rations, housing and other social privileges. Until 1936, when Joseph Stalin announced that Soviet society had purportedly achieved socialism, the state used disenfranchizing as a constitutional measure aimed at marginalizing the "class-alien" groups of population, including "exploiters," clergy and "people not engaged in labor." The Jews had a singularly high proportion of second-class citizens with curtailed rights.[4]

While separate and clusters of agrarian settlements helped in solving economic and social problems by building a "productive" segment of the Jewish population, Communist leaders had a bigger idea of fully "normalizing" the Jews as a distinct Soviet nation by providing them with a proper territory in the multi-ethnic patchwork of the USSR. Projects of creating a Jewish territory, including a hybrid Belorussian-Jewish republic, were propounded in the early years after the revolution. In the most popular blueprint of the mid-1920s, the main building site for a Jewish republic was supposed to be in northern areas of the Crimean Peninsula. Ultimately, the attention turned to the vast area east of the Ural Mountains dividing the European and Asian (Siberian) parts of country. Before 1917 only a limited number of Jews could put down roots there and form communities. Among those Jews were former convicts, because the tsarist state widely used Siberia as a place of exile and imprisonment. Now Birobidzhan—an area in the Siberian Far East—should become the place for building a Jewish national home. The Birobidzhan project under discussion in this book was inaugurated in 1928 with the aim of building *ex nihilo* a Jewish territorial unit five thousand miles east from Moscow.

The promotion of national territories and languages was the major positive feature of the Soviet nationalities policy, especially in the first two decades after the revolution. Although Vladimir Lenin and Joseph Stalin (the latter considered to be the main expert on nationalities) denounced federation in their pre-1917 writings and advocated a unitary state with territory units for national regions, the term *federation* was rehabilitated later, and the Soviet Union was constitutionally shaped as such. In reality, the ethnofederal structure formed a façade for a heavily centralized state, leaving very little decision-making power to the constituent authorities.[5]

Birobidzhan was conceived as a hitherto missing component in the complex territorial structure, built to reflect the multi-ethnic mosaic of the country. This, as well as attempts to solve economic and social problems of disadvantaged groups among the Jews living in the former Pale, were the main objectives of the Soviet leadership. The project, initiated by the government rather than by Jewish activists, also purported to redefine Soviet Jews as a Birobidzhan-centered secular nation, only tangentially related to the Jewish communities in other countries. Soviet ideology tabooed the concept of a world Jewish nation as reactionary, nationalist and Zionist. From the very beginning of the Far Eastern project, the Soviet propaganda machinery emphasized its importance for creating a positive counterbalance to the Zionist endeavor in Palestine. This propaganda line was echoed by foreign observers with a pro-Soviet orientation.

While resettlement campaigns were part of the reconstruction undertaken by the Soviet state,[6] the Jewish resettlement in the European part of the country and to the Far East differed by drawing particularly close attention and even involvement from foreign organizations, from time to time becoming a factor in international relations. Historians, writers, journalists and memoirists of various countries described the Soviet Jewish territorial unit in numerous book-length treatments.[7]

Pure objectivity was sparse in journalist and some academic writings about Birobidzhan. The project's ambitious ideological agenda and its heavily slanted appraisal by politically engaged pundits often eclipsed the lackluster and sometimes tragic reality of what was going on in a highly remote and least-developed area of the country. At the same time, ideologically opposing outlets tended to suspect alternative motives in the Far Eastern project, presenting it as a device for anti-Jewish oppression. Some publications and documentaries stressed the "exoticism" of setting: wild forests, bitterly cold winters, Red Book Amur tigers, the geographical remoteness from Moscow and proximity of the Chinese border.

This book focuses upon the origin and evolution of the Birobidzhan project, seeing as a product and quintessence of the Soviet state's policy towards its Jews as well as part of the general nationalities policy. Newly accessible archival sources, innumerable electronically stored pages of periodicals and books, and recent publications, notably by scholars based in Birobidzhan and other cities in Russia's Far East, allow to reconstruct in more detail and precision the ambitious endeavor that stalled from the very beginning, but left a non-negligible trace in the Jewish history of the 20th century. Although the newly minted Jewish "homeland" never had attracted for settlement any sizable titular population and generally remained a remote economic and cultural backwater, it played a notable role in the history of Soviet Jews and, particularly in the 1930s, gained enthusiastic (and sometimes delusional) endorsement or at least close attention from various quarters of the international community. A relic of the project, the Jewish Autonomous Region with the city of Birobidzhan as its center, still exists on the map of Russia as an anachronistic territorial artifact of Soviet ethnic experiments.

CHAPTER 1
THE SPECTER OF A JEWISH REPUBLIC

On March 28, 1928, the Central Executive Committee, which acted as the country's governing body in the interims of the sessions of the All-Union Congress of Soviets, constitutionally the highest organ of state power, announced its decision to start a campaign of Jewish resettlement to the Russian Far East. During the mid-1920s to mid-1930s, some form of territorial autonomy was granted to most of the various Soviet nationalities. The Far Eastern project was not exclusively focused on establishing Jewish agricultural communities. Still, the vision of an ex-shtetl dweller transformed into a farmer played presumably a large, if not determining, role in the decision makers' thinking process.

Agricultural colonization was in itself an old idea on how to make Jews "productive" and generally "normal." In the 19th century, this line of thinking and acting led the tsarist government to establishing colonies in Novorossiya (New Russia), the then name of the region north of the Black Sea and now in the southeast of Ukraine. "Colony" was the appellation used in Imperial Russia and then in the early Soviet Union for new villages of settlers, who were often non-Slavic. The Jewish colonies were the only ones populated by non-Christian settlers.

Although the number of Jewish farmers was relatively few (by the end of the 19th century, about 60,000 lived in over two hundred colonies),[1] this did not mean that all other Russian Jews were completely detached from agriculture. It was not unusual for shtetl dwellers to have their own cows, goats and horses and to keep at least a few chickens. *Yishuvniks*, or isolated Jewish families within non-Jewish villages, such as the household of Sholem Aleichem's Tevye the dairyman, formed a separate category of east European

Jews. Thousands of Jews made a living by trading in agricultural commodities. Moyshe Olgin, a Jewish journalist and political activist, wrote that in his native shtetl of Buki, now in Cherkasy Region of Ukraine, in one way or another "each and every Jew lived of land."[2] So, for some it was not impossibly challenging to become directly engaged in agricultural activities.

In the Soviet institutional network, two agencies carried responsibility for Jewish colonization: the governmental Committee for the Settlement of Toiling Jews on the Land (KOMZET), appointed in August 1924, and the purportedly nongovernmental voluntary Association for the Settlement of Toiling Jews on the Land (OZET), established in January 1925. As an anomaly in the Soviet Jewish history, they were the only long-existing, centralized bodies operating throughout the USSR. Both became the government's liaisons to the Jewish population and foreign sponsors, pursuing the objective of finding a useful and self-supporting occupation for at least part of the economically disengaged and socially alienated shtetl dwellers. Subsequently, the Jewish agricultural activity, initially a decentralized grassroots phenomenon, took the shape of a state-run campaign aimed at not only solving economic woes but also harmonizing the social structure of the Jewish population. The OZET published its journal, *Tribuna* (Tribune, 1927–1937[3]), which came out in Russian and thus stressed the all-Soviet, rather than exclusively Jewish, character and objectives of the campaign. Otherwise, the state defined as "Jewish" only such forms of journalism, literature, education and theater which were associated with Yiddish or with the languages of the smaller non-Ashkenazic Jewish groups in Central Asia, Crimea and the Caucasus.

The objective of having a peasant class, which was common for Jewish activists of various ideological hues, had found a place also in the Bolshevik nationalities theory, formulated prominently by Stalin. As early as 1913, he stated that the lack of a toiling peasantry rooted in a territory of their own forestalled the formation of the Jews as a nation.[4] In 1926, Malka Frumkin (aka Esther), a former Jewish socialist turned influential Soviet functionary and one of the leading figures in the Jewish Sections of the Communist Party, claimed to have a clear vision of the path to the future of the Soviet Jewry. Her strategy of social transformation did not concern proletarians and other productive cohorts of the Jewish population. It was taken for granted that they could easily get or had already procured a foothold in mainstream socialist society. Frumkin focused on the "non-productive elements," those unable to eke out a living in the precarious economy of their shtetls. Many of them were to be compactly settled in rural areas, where they could eventually remold and consolidate to form a socialist Jewish nation.[5]

Around the same time forty-eight Soviet Yiddish writers put their signatures under an open letter published on April 15, 1926, in the Moscow Yiddish daily *Der Emes* (Truth). They called on their foreign colleagues in America and Europe to assist in enacting the plan of Jewish settlement and thus make true the dream of the classics of Yiddish literature—Mendele Moykher Sforim, Sholem Aleichem and Itskhok Leybush Peretz—about transforming the Jewish market petty dealers and good-for-nothings into self-supporting, socially useful citizens.

Productivization through agriculture, an abiding fixation not only of the tsarist officialdom, but also of Jewish intellectuals and philanthropists, found enthusiastic support even among those foreign activists and pundits who did not belong to openly pro-Soviet circles. Baruch Glasman, an American Yiddish prose writer, explained this enthusiasm: "It is a great joy for all of us, because here, too, our life is being normalized, because a peasant class is being created among Jews—and not only in the Soviet Union but among the whole Jewish people; a peasant class that must bring new freshness and new content into our lives."[6]

Productivization clicked well with the leadership of the American Jewish Joint Distribution Committee (JDC), which originated in the wake of World War I and developed into a large, influential aid organization with an international scope of operations. Boris Bogen, who headed the European operations of the JDC, had heretofore worked as principal of the Baron de Hirsch Trade School, in Woodbine, New Jersey, established to provide agricultural training for east European immigrants. Joseph Rosen, who represented the JDC in the

Soviet Union, was a noted agronomist. His "Rosen rye," a variety of winter crop, had been grown widely in the United States. In July 1924, the JDC set in motion an operation under the name of the American Jewish Joint Agricultural Corporation (Agro-Joint), whose main brief was to supervise the resettlement of Soviet Jews on farming colonies.[7]

Both Bogen and Rosen were Moscow natives who had successfully integrated into American society after leaving tsarist Russia for political reasons. Both believed that Russian Jewry had a strong potential for social and economic development. In 1917, Bogen wrote that in Russia "the Jews, notwithstanding political restrictions and persecutions, do not represent the lowest strata of society, and ... in the matter of education, art, and morals, the Jews stand very much higher than the peasants and city workers."[8]

The scope and budget of the Agro-Joint were discussed in September 1925 during a conference convened under the aegis of the JDC in Philadelphia with participation of over a thousand communal leaders, philanthropists and social workers. The (non-Jewish) veteran revolutionary Pyotr Smidovich, who headed the KOMZET, sent a welcoming address to the conference, stating that "the Soviet government never doubted the soundness of the plan to transfer a considerable part of the Jewish population in Soviet Russia to agricultural work." However, the government could not supply the large sums of money required for enacting this plan. Therefore, the KOMZET reckoned greatly on support of foreign Jewish organizations and promised them "full freedom of action."

The response to the Soviet Jewish colonization campaign was widely positive despite forceful criticism levelled by the Zionists. Even the largest New York Yiddish daily, *Forverts* (with a circulation of a quarter of a million copies), which was right-socialist and did not spare broadsides to the Soviet regime, called its readers to participate in raising money for the unprecedented, challenging project. Some American socialists imagined a demarcation line separating the Communist movement from the Soviet regime, regarding the latter as essentially socialist in its economic and social policy choices and cherishing an illusion that it would ultimately acquire democratic credentials.[9] A variety of motives, most notably humanitarian, anti-Zionist or simply pro-Soviet ones, led a broad range of sponsors to support the Agro-Joint. Julius Rosenwald, a businessmen and philanthropist, pledged one million dollars (over 16 million in purchasing power of a century later) for Soviet colonization, while Felix M. Warburg, a banker and the JDC chairman, pledged a matching donation.[10]

Sholem Asch, a bestselling Yiddish writer and one of the founders of the JDC, spent two weeks surveying Jewish colonies in Crimea and Ukraine in 1928, which happened to be a bad harvest year. Nonetheless, the guest came back carrying a positive impression from what he had seen. The colonists with whom he spoke appeared satisfied with their conditions of life and thanked the state and the foreign sponsors for the help they had provided. Asch promised to inform American Jews that every cent, invested by them into the Soviet projects, had been used for good causes. He expressed hope that the Jewish colonization would impede assimilation and facilitate preservation of Yiddish. He also visited several shtetls, where he found Jews who vegetated in misery being ill-equipped to find a place in the new order. Asch, who "could be a Bundist [Jewish socialist] in the morning and a Zionist in the evening," said that by the end of his Soviet sojourn he turned into an "almost hundred-percent Communist."[11]

The Soviet Jewish colonization project appealed to both existing and specially newly established organizations in many countries. Of great significance was the involvement of the ORT, a Russian acronym for the Organization for the Distribution of Artisanal and Agricultural Skills among the Jews, initially configured in 1880 in St Petersburg. In 1921, the first post-war conference of the ORT was convened in Berlin, transforming the hitherto Russian organization into the World ORT Union. A division of labor between the JDC and the ORT had been of great benefit to the colonization project. The ORT leadership was dominated by erstwhile Jewish Territorialists, whose program developed as an outgrowth of Zionism but envisaged building a Yiddish (rather than Hebrew) speaking Jewish state outside Palestine. So, non-Zionist colonization projects generally appealed to former and current Territorialists. Less than six months before he died in August 1926, Israel Zangwill, a popular British novelist and the father of Territorialism, took part in a meeting held in support of the Jewish colonization campaign in Russia.[12]

To many Jewish activists, the Soviet Union of the mid-1920s appeared a happier place than Palestine. Devotees of Yiddish were happy that the state recognized and sponsored their cherished language, spoken then by millions of Jews worldwide, rather than the "bourgeois-cum-clerical" Hebrew, which had been in practice if not by law suppressed in the Soviet Union. Until 1938, Yiddish enjoyed the status of being one of the state languages in Belorussia and was widely used in Ukraine. Teachers' training colleges and university departments turned out an ever-growing cadre for hundreds of Yiddish schools, including vocational ones. Scores of scholars worked at the Kyiv-based Institute for Jewish Proletarian Culture of the Ukrainian Academy of Sciences and at the Jewish Department of the Belorussian Academy of Sciences. In 1927–35, five Jewish national districts were established in Ukraine and Crimea.

The colonization drive developed in the climate of the New Economic Policy (NEP), crafted to (temporarily) give a place to private enterprise and bourgeois class. As a result, the economy, which had undergone severe convulsions following the world and civil wars, and the break of the imperial system, began to recover at a rapid pace. Some people regarded Stalin as a moderately authoritarian and a fairly enlightened leader and did not realize that he was already backsliding on the liberalization of the early NEP period. In 1926, Abraham Cahan, editor of *Forverts*, welcomed the victory of Stalin and his group over their opponents, including Leon Trotsky. According to Cahan's delusional analysis, this was a promising development that augured improvements in the Soviet government's relationship with the socialist movement and the country's entry into the democratic fold.[13] Austrian journalist and writer Joseph Roth, one of the numerous pilgrims to the Soviet Union, wrote in 1926:

> Today Soviet Russia is the only country in Europe where anti-Semitism is scorned, though it might not have ceased. Jews are entirely free citizens—though their freedom may not yet signify that a solution of the Jewish question is at hand. As individuals

they are free from hatred and persecution. As a people they have *all* the rights of a "national minority." In the history of the Jews, such a sudden and complete liberation is unexampled.[14]

In November 1926, Jewish activists were in seventh heaven when a speech by Mikhail Kalinin, chairman of the All-Union Executive Committee and thus the (largely ceremonial) head of the Soviet state, contained pronouncements that could be construed as a tentative promise to form a Jewish republic in Crimea. Henceforth, Kalinin, who in his writings and statements also railed against anti-Semitism, garnered admiration from Jews all over the world. An American functionary of the JDC wrote a decade later, "Not a Jew, he has been one of the men who from the beginning believed that a bent Jewish peddler could be transformed into a horny-handed farmer."[15]

Theories were put forward about the beneficial effects of agricultural work, particularly for overcoming the perceived debilitating psychological and physical traits of shtetl Jewry. Nikolai Semashko, People's Commissar (Minister) of Health in 1918–1930, referred to the physical transformation of Jewish farmers in an article entitled "New Person is Being Born." He noted that Jews in agricultural colonies completely changed their style of walking, talking and comporting themselves. Thus, "instead of the quick, nervous machine-gun speech peculiar to the Jews of tsarist Russia," they spoke with Semashko "in the confident, deliberate and clear voice."[16]

For all that, the resettlement to agricultural colonies did not fully dominate the Soviet authorities' strategy chosen for resolving the Jewish issue. Many more small towns' Jewish dwellers were involved in two other processes: first, migration to urban industrial centers and, second, transformation of the shtetls, which were reluctantly acknowledged as a reality of Jewish life in the socialist country. In 1925, the ideology-driven bureaucracy in Ukraine, with a stroke of the pen, removed the shtetl (*mestechko* in Russian) from Soviet maps, because in the country of the hammer and sickle it was more appropriate to define these settlements as "towns/cities," "villages" and—a term coined in the mid-1920s—"urban-type settlements" (*poselki gorodskogo tipa*).[17] In Belorussia, only several scores of small towns remained categorized as shtetls in the official administrative and territorial structure of the republic until 1938.[18] Whether it was rebranded or not, the shtetl stubbornly functioned as the place where rural and urban, Jewish and non-Jewish components of the economy interacted, trying to survive—and somehow survived until the Holocaust or even later—in the Soviet environment.

By the end of the 1920s the situation had changed from that of a decade earlier. First of all, outmigration, particularly of young people, eased the shtetl problem. The Jewish population in the shtetls, including the rebranded ones, had declined to half a million, or under a fifth of all Soviet Jews.[19] Several decrees issued by the central and republican Soviet governments allocated funds to building new factories in the areas inhabited by Jews and to helping Jewish artisans organize their producers' cooperatives. These developments created jobs in former shtetls for many of those who had passed up a chance to move to cities or colonies. Professionally qualified people could work in educational and cultural institutions, in hospitals, and in the local state and Party apparatus.

Itsik Fefer, a leading Yiddish poet in Ukraine, admired numerous signs of profound changes in his home shtetl of Shpola: a club for workers of the clothing industry, new houses and a tannery that provided jobs for local workers. The former dive-keeper traded in needlework rather than in liquor and girls, and her only son was in the Red Army. The poet's onetime religious teacher died, and his daughter eloped with a non-Jewish man. The synagogue sexton dreamt about a position of a courier at the local Party committee. In all, not very much was left of the old shtetl, of the "synagogue, goats, shops and mud."[20] A new hybrid—"Soviet-and-kosher" (as Anna Shternshis termed it)— Jewish life took root in a shtetl. It was a predominantly Yiddish-speaking world where a ritual butcher could continue to ply his trade in an all-Jewish craft-based cooperative or state-owned abattoir. Yet, the only way he and his pious colleagues knew to slaughter fowl and beef cattle was to do it in the kosher manner. Thus, "Soviet meat turned out to be kosher."[21] Children reared on "Soviet-and-kosher" food would finish a local Yiddish school and then move to a city for education or work, leaving the parochial world of their parents behind.

The situation in the country changed radically in 1928. This year marked the transition from the quasi-market economy of the NEP to the fully centralized, command economy system of the First Five-Year Plan, aimed at rapid industrialization, general economic advancement of the country and removing the remaining bourgeois element from the structure of Soviet society. Zakhar Mindlin, a high-ranking Soviet statistician, contended that the introduction of the Five-Year Plan would improve Jewish life in the country. According to his prognosis, in 1933 the Jewish unemployment would decline to a minimum level and Jewish traders would be totally wiped out, whereas the number of Jewish workers would reach 350,000. His optimistic prognosis did not convince Ezekiel Groer (sometimes spelled Grower), a lawyer and economist who served as a vice-president of Agro-Joint. Groer was skeptical about the prospects of Jewish economic reconstruction and envisioned instead a "Jewish economic funeral."[22]

Indeed, by reducing the private sector of the economy, the government increased the number of Jews compelled to seek alternative sources of income. By various estimates, between 350,000 and over 900,000 Jews were left in economic distress.[23] The colonization project in the European part of the country could contribute little to solving a problem of this scale. The presupposed republic-in-the-making in Crimea and the colonies in other areas had limited territorial resources for scaling up the resettlement and absorbing the excess shtetl population. Two more things constricted the expansion of the projects in the European part of the country. First, the projects were set in contested territories. The Tatars regarded the Crimea peninsula as their ancestral land, while competition for land led to tension and even conflicts between Jewish and Ukrainian farmers, and to carefully orchestrated resistance of Ukraine's functionaries.[24] Second, the lopsided—almost exclusively agricultural—character of the economy in the areas of Jewish colonization. For all that, the convincing success of agricultural colonization had proved that the resettlement of shtetl dwellers could bring practical results and, thanks to substantial foreign aid, did not involve excessively burdensome investments. Moreover, it contributed to fostering international relations.[25]

Several expeditions to sparsely inhabited areas of the country explored the feasibility of building a Jewish republic *ex nihilo*, which was in contrast to all other Soviet ethnic territorial units, created more or less in the boundaries of the titular nationality's historical settlement. In 1928, the choice fell on a territory over five thousand miles from Moscow—in a southern area of the Far East, historically a part of Manchuria, annexed from China in 1858–1860. Reinforcement of the region, whose borders remained porous to illegal trade including drugs (opium) and migration, was a weighty factor in making the decision. One can only second-guess what the Moscow decision makers considered more important: to assign the Far Eastern outskirts for Jewish nation-building, or rather to attract the Jews and the Jews-related international help to buttress the infrastructure and economy of a remote, underpopulated and underdeveloped area.

Initial reports about the new Jewish settlement project pointed to Bureya, the area named after one of the largest tributaries of the Amur River, the chief waterway in that corner of country. In fact, Bureya was adjacent to the stretch designated for Jewish settlement and later rarely appeared in the press reports, whereas a different geographical name was coined and re-coined to define the region in question: initially it was hyphenated as Birsko-Bidzhan, then Biro-Bidzhan or Bira/Biro-Bidjan, and finally solidified as Birobidjan or Birobidzhan. For some time, the name was rendered as Birebidzhan in Yiddish. The toponym came from the names of two other tributaries of the Amur River—the Bira and the Bidzhan. Inadvertently, it rhymed well with some other Soviet constituents, such as Uzbekistan and Azerbaijan. The name "Bira" and "Bidzhan" come from the Tungusic language spoken by one of the small indigenous groups in the area living from hunting and fishing.

In its final boundaries the area has the size of the contemporary Republic of China, or Taiwan (36,000 sq. km or 13,895 sq. miles), though initially it would usually be compared with the somewhat smaller Belgium or with even smaller territories of the Crimean Peninsula and Palestine. By 1928, the entire population of Birobidzhan was around thirty thousand, mainly Russians, including Amur Cossacks, and a smaller number of Koreans. This population figure took in a couple of thousand non-Jewish settlers who came to the area, above all from Ukraine and Belorussia, in the 20th century. The Cossacks, or Slavic peasants-cum-warriors, whose parents or foreparents had settled along the borders by the orders of the imperial administration, fled in great numbers to China following the post-1917 civil war in which they sided with anti-Bolshevik forces. Koreans had begun to migrate to the Russian Far East in the 1860s, fleeing the famine in their home country. The nearest Jewish community was in the city of Khabarovsk, where Jews, initially several families of privileged retired soldiers, made their home in the 1880s onwards.[26]

The March 1928 announcement of assigning a territory for Jewish settlement in the Far East, which made headlines around the world, did not come completely out of the blue. In January and February, the press heralded the news of a government-backed plan to resettle hundreds of thousands of Jews in Siberia.[27] According to Abram Merezhin, a leading functionary of OZET and KOMZET, the Birsko-Bidzhan area could ultimately home as many as a million people directly or indirectly engaged in agriculture and industry.[28] The Jewish Telegraphic Agency, headquartered in New York with correspondents worldwide including in Moscow, referred to the statements by a top figure in OZET, Samuel (Shmuel) Weizmann, whose brother, Chaim Weizmann, the future first President of Israel, lived in Manchester at that time, combining his university work with acting as President of the World Zionist Organization. Samuel Weizmann declared that the remoteness of the region could not deter Jews from going there. Dire economic conditions in the erstwhile Pale of Jewish Settlement would push them to seek a better life in the back of beyond of the Far East. On the basis of this expectation, it was planned to settle ten thousand Jewish families in the designated area by the end of the five-year period. Weizmann stressed that a gigantic task laid ahead, especially as the Far Eastern climatic conditions of hot humid summers and freezing winters differed dramatically from those in Crimea, located between the temperate and subtropical climate belts.[29]

Zalman Wendroff, a Yiddish author who then acted as the Moscow correspondent of *Forverts*, echoed the belief that the distant location should not represent a serious disadvantage. He pointed out that

Russian Jews were not afraid to travel as far as to Uruguay, Cuba and Mexico, where they had to learn a foreign language and, generally, accommodate themselves to local culture. Significantly, the Far Eastern area was rich of water (a dearth of which seriously complicated the situation in Crimean colonies), its land was fertile for farming, and there was a good opportunity to build "a purely Jewish settlement." Furthermore, as Wendroff claimed without leaving Moscow, the locals had no qualms about welcoming Jewish migrants.[30] He might have gleaned this encouraging information from a travelogue published in the mass circulation Russian-language weekly magazine *Ogonek* (Little Flame). Angela Rohr, a German journalist who lived in Moscow and in 1928 visited Bira-Bishan (as the magazine spelled the novel toponym), wrote about the local Russians' friendly attitude to all newcomers.[31]

The presence of Amur Cossacks in the area raised troubling questions. The word "Cossack" had connotations of anti-Jewish violence in the past (massacres conducted by the Ukrainian insurgents in the 17th century) and more recently (pogroms in late Imperial Russia and during the civil war). However, following his trip to the Far East in April 1928, Merezhin had concluded too that neither the Russians nor the Koreans were prone to anti-Semitism. According to his observation, historical allusions had nothing at all to do with the Cossacks of the Far East. He described them as "primitive" but honest and open people, who kept their word and did not steal. The newly arrived Jews gave him more worries, which might point to his ethnic self-hatred, a rather common trait among Jewish socialists.[32] He argued that the arriving settlers had "a different past, a different upbringing and, as a result, a different character and a different kind of attitude to other people." Merezhin found it appalling that some of them would call a non-Jew names—such as *der khazer* (the pig)—without any provocation.[33]

In the event, aggressive antipathy towards Jews did not become a particularly serious issue among the local inhabitants, though in the end it was not entirely negligible.[34] Menachem Kadyshevich, a Soviet chronicler of the Birobidzhan project, posited that the locals were indeed "much less than in other places of the Soviet Union intoxicated with the venom of old prejudices." He remarked, nonetheless, that "miracles do not happen in general and in Birobidzhan in particular," especially as part of the population was made up of migrants from Ukraine, who tended to have unamiable views of Jews.[35]

Lack of anti-Semitism became a key propaganda claim. Alexander Troyanovsky, the Soviet ambassador appointed after the US finally recognized the Soviet regime in 1933, travelled to America via the Far East and made a stop in Birobidzhan. Later he wrote: "The most pleasant observation in my survey of Biro-Bidjan was the exceptionally friendly relationship between the Jews and the local Russian population."[36] Claims that Birobidzhan was void of anti-Semitism recur also in sources having nothing to do with propaganda.[37]

As for Merezhin's assurances that the locals would welcome the Jews, they smacked of the common Zionist (and colonialist) claim of a civilizing mission carried out by "culturally superior" settlers.[38] His statements generally echoed the vocabulary of the Zionist movement to which he belonged before 1917. Merezhin declared, for instance, that the chief aim in the new project was not merely to create a Jewish region similar to a Jewish district in Ukraine, but "a Jewish territory," and he doubted if without the slogan "On to the Jewish land!" the Jewish settlers would have come and remained in the Far East.[39] This slogan appeared as the title of an article by Alexander Chemeriski, the head of the Party's Jewish Sections, published in *Der Emes* on January 22, 1928 as the first official signal of the Birobidzhan campaign. Merezhin was then in Minsk, where he became so enthused with the project of building a Jewish republic in the Soviet Union that in his public address, he paraphrased "If you will, it is no dream"—Theodor Herzl's words turned into a slogan of the Zionist movement.[40]

Nathan Chanin, an influential figure among American Jewish socialists, travelled in the Soviet Union in 1928 and reported *inter alia* that Soviet experts and activists generally averted speaking about Birobidzhan. Some of them, however, told him that they considered the government-conceived campaign an irresponsible, needless diversion from deepening the success achieved in Ukraine and Crimea, and that Jews were mainly reluctant to participate in the resettling.[41] Some Jewish Communists, including former members of

Jewish political groups, took literally the last line of Karl Marx and Friedrich Engels's 1948 Communist Manifesto calling for international proletarian unity—"Workers of the world, unite!"—and looked askance at the "nationalist" idea of building a separate Jewish polity.

No doubt, the decision to allocate a territory for Jewish settlement could not be taken without Stalin's consent, though quite when and how it had been obtained remains unclear. In any case, publicly the Birobidzhan project was associated with Kalinin rather than directly with Stalin, which left the whole undertaking more open to criticism even by Soviet functionaries. Yurii Larin (born as Ikhil-Mikhl Lurie), a veteran revolutionary who was a proponent of the Crimean project and chaired the OZET, made no secret of his view of Birobidzhan as a place unsuitable for agricultural colonization. He listed such deterrents as the permanently frozen subsoil, marsh-ridden terrain, floods, prolonged frosts, cultural isolation, unbearable intensity of labor, short growing period under unfavorable seasonal distribution of precipitation, and bloodsucking insects, known as *gnus*.[42]

It is hard to find a description of the Birobidzhan area without mentioning of the woes caused by clouds of omnipresent insects, whose only virtue was that they did not carry human diseases. Judging by Angela Rohr's experience, "mosquitos and biting flies were the true masters of that land," giving people a rest only between midnight and 4 o'clock in the morning. By contrast, the American National Geographical Society responded to the news about the Birobidzhan project with a description aimed at ruining the stereotypical vision of Siberia as a dreary, treeless waste fit only for prisoners moving in long lines across bleak naked landscapes, where their ranks being decimated by wild animals and the cruel treatment of the guards. "Much of the scenery along the Amur River may achieve notoriety for its wild beauty when the country is better known to the world at large."[43]

Crucially, however, the Far Eastern project failed writ large to engender the same spread of enthusiastic excitement among foreign sponsors as the Crimean project. Most consequential was the JDC's disinterest in sponsoring the new enterprise. Joseph Rosen did not hide his puzzlement and disappointment about Moscow's decision to give a green light to a proposal which had not been sufficiently examined. He had serious doubts that the distant area fit for Jewish colonization. Above all, the existing colonization projects in the European part of the country were far from being completed.[44] Later Rosen issued a more careful statement, clarifying that he by no means regarded the Birobidzhan project as undesirable or dangerous, but rather as a plan which, conducted by the Soviet government, might be favorable, although he did not have the facts at hand to evaluate the merits of it.[45]

Meanwhile, the stock-market crash in 1929 debilitated American Jewry's ability to support humanitarian projects in other countries. The income of the JDC had declined from 3.5 million dollars in 1928 to 1.6 million in 1929 and less than 1.2 million in 1930. The Depression produced the demands for focusing above all on domestic relief. Rosen noted that even though conditions were not very good in the Soviet Union, the situation of people whom he met in his American abode, Croton-on-the-Hudson, was even worse.[46] The ORT was also badly affected by a worldwide economic depression, but found an alternative source of help in the prosperous Jewish community in South Africa.[47] Even so, the ORT, which worked in conjunction with the JDC, balked at being involved in the Far Eastern endeavor.

Against this backdrop, various foreign pro-Soviet organizations threw their support behind the new project. The Organization for Jewish Colonization in Russia, or ICOR, formed in the United States in 1924 by a group of Communists and later spread to Canada, was the most effective of such sponsors.[48] Thus, in March 1929, the ICOR sent to Birobidzhan a transport of tractors, machines, motors and tools worth $55,000.[49] In Argentina, Uruguay and Brazil, enthusiasts of Birobidzhan contributed to the organization called PROCOR.[50] The Soviet representative, Yankel (Jacob) Levin, who visited Argentina in 1929, next year took up the post of chairman of the Communist Party Committee in the just-established Birobidzhan District. In 1934, the Latvian authorities closed the OSEK, which united the supporters of Birobidzhan, and its journal *Nayerd* (New Land).[51] Still, similar bodies continued their activities in other countries.

In Poland, the short-lived organization Agro-Yid was established in June 1934 and closed by authorities in 1935. The Polish Ministry of the

Interior prohibited distribution of the newspaper *Birobidzhaner Shtern* (Birobidzhan Star), published in Birobidzhan from 1930. Established in 1930 as a bilingual—Yiddish and Russian—publication, it later split into two newspapers. The title of the Russian newspaper, *Birobidzhanskaia Zvezda*, had the same meaning of "Birobidzhan star." The Agro-Yid's chairman, Michael Suritz, was a relative of Jacob Suritz, the Soviet envoy to Germany in 1934–37.[52]

From the very beginning, Birobidzhan was juxtaposed with Palestine. In addition to purely dogmatic motives, anti-Zionist propaganda had practical objectives. A negative image of life in Palestine should dissuade Soviet citizens from moving to the Middle Eastern site of Jewish nation-building. This was not a negligible stream of emigrants, amounting around 10,000 in 1924–27.[53] Anti-Zionist broadsides were also aimed at foreign Jewish circles, inducing them to fundraise in favor of the Soviet rather than the Zionist projects.

In June 1928, that is three months after the announcement of the Birobidzhan project, the Soviet authorities closed arguably the last remaining independent political party in the country—the Jewish Communist Workers Party (Poale Zion). This party had broken off from the Labor Zionist mainstream and closely aligned with the Bolsheviks but disagreed with their position on the Jewish question. Principally, it saw a national territorial solution only in Palestine.[54] Foreign Zionists were more vociferous in opposing the Soviet project, arguing that "it diverted Jewish money and Jewish hope from the Homeland to just a country of the exile."[55]

In his 1929 pamphlet *Birobidzhan and Palestina*, Isaac Sudarsky, an agronomist and a functionary in Ukraine's OZET, polemicized with the Zionists engaged in building "a Jewish pseudo-utopian state in Palestine" and described the advantages of Birobidzhan, particularly its richness of mineral resources. Most importantly, while "the Zionists use ideology to lure the Jewish proletariat into the holy land, Birobidzhan does not require any ideological support. Its climate, rich soils and prominent agricultural potential speak for themselves." In Sudarsky's reasoning, the Zionist project had no future, because it was "founded on one nation oppressing the other," whereas Birobidzhan developed as an all-Soviet project, where Jews and non-Jews together were called and mobilized "to develop as fast as possible this extremely rich region."[56]

Tellingly, the OZET was configured and run not as a Jewish organization, but rather as an association of Soviet citizens with a brief to realize the state's directive concerning the Jews. Moreover, its membership—123,000 in 1928 and 250,000 in 1930—was increasingly non-Jewish.[57] When Sholem Asch came to Moscow in 1928, the governing body of OZET found a way of putting the guest to good use by inviting him to take part in the drawing ceremony of OZET's lottery, whose tickets could be purchased all over the country. Addressing the audience, Asch said inter alia that it was his first-time experience to face a Jewish event whose participants were both Jews and non-Jews.[58]

In his memoirs, Chaim Weizmann quoted his mother's words that "whatever happens, I shall be well off. If Samuel is right, we shall be happy in Russia, and if Chaim is right, then I shall go to live in Palestine."[59] Indeed, not having a crystal ball to tell what the future held, many people believed that a project developed by the Soviet state had a better chance of success than the Zionist enterprise in the Middle East, which encountered resistance from the local population and the British administration. In addition, not a few Jewish cultural activists looked "with great fear at the new, alien tribe that" was "being created, before our very eyes, in Palestine."[60] Meanwhile, some particularly skeptical foreign observers were not sure which of the two Weizmann brothers had a wilder imagination.[61]

CHAPTER 2
GROWING PAINS

From the very beginning, the process of building Birobidzhan was slow and haphazard. In May 1928 the first group of intrepid settlers brought a spark of new life into the railway hamlet of Tikhonkaya, whose name aptly meant "tranquil one" in Russian: it had a population of around eight (in some sources six) hundred people of various ethnicities, including Russians, Germans, Estonians, Poles, Chinese, Koreans, Chuvashs and Mordvins. Built in 1912, the station would sell on average only a couple of tickets a day.[1] After 1928, the sleepy hamlet began to transform into the main hub of the settlement project, though initially the center of the area began to take shape about thirty miles from Tikhonkaya and got the name of Birofeld ("Biro Field" in Yiddish). Birofeld housed the first Jewish local council (soviet), the first Yiddish school and the first local Yiddish newspaper *Birofeld Emes* (Birofeld Truth). However, it was a transient "capital": when the area received the status of a district, Tikhonkaya rather than Birofeld became its center.[2] The term "colony" was little used in the Far East for denoting new villages. In 1929, a village named Nayfeld ("New Field") grew up less than twenty miles from Birofeld. Both villages still exist.

In contrast with the Kalinindorf Jewish National District already in existence since 1927 and the Jewish districts established in later years in Ukraine (Nayzlatopol in 1929 and Stalindorf in 1931) and in Crimea (Fraydorf in 1930 and Larindorf in 1935), the words "Jewish National" were curiously missing in the name of the Birobidzhan District when it appeared on the Soviet map in August 1930. This omission was by no means accidental. It clearly indicated that the Moscow decision makers remained uncertain of how the project might go and did not bet everything on Birobidzhan. The 1928 resolution of the Central Executive Committee carried a guarded wording about a "possibility of organizing a Jewish national administrative-territorial entity in case of promising results of migration of Jewish workers to the area."[3]

Max Kiper, who chaired the Party's Jewish Sections in Ukraine, wrote in 1929 that, notwithstanding the campaign of resettlement to Birobidzhan, the *main work* continued to proceed in Ukraine, Crimea and Belorussia.[4] Upward of two thousand families moved to Crimean colonies in 1929 and, overall, the Jewish agricultural settlement work in Crimea received significantly stronger support in the state budget allocations in the coming couple of years.[5] It is worth mentioning that the entire program of settling Jews on land and engaging them in agricultural labor developed incongruously with the concurrently dominant pattern of migration from villages to expanding cities and towns. Not only geographically, but also on the scale of economic and political importance, the Birobidzhan project remained somewhere in an obscure periphery of the dynamic landscape of the Five-Year Plan. The Far Eastern site of Jewish nation-building was highly praised in the press, but little attended to practically. The first settlers had to work at logging in the *taiga* (Siberian forests) to earn enough money to keep them afloat until making their agricultural endeavors successful.[6]

In 1934, the New York Yiddish journalist Ben Zion Goldberg, a son-in-law of Sholem Aleichem and (at that time) a great enthusiast of Birobidzhan, revealed "the secret of the excellent progress" in developing the Far Eastern project: "instead of being built up by Jews in what we call a typical Jewish manner" (sic!), Birobidzhan was "reclaimed with that Soviet efficiency which came into play in the construction of Dnieperstroi and Magnitogorsk."[7] Goldberg referred to the large-scale constructions of the then world's largest Dnieper Hydroelectric Station, in Ukraine, and of the one-industry town of Magnitogorsk, in the Urals, modelled after the American steel-producing cities Gary, Indiana, and Pittsburgh, Pennsylvania. They were designed and built by Soviet and American specialists. So were numerous other industrial projects. Despite Goldberg's claims, nothing of this kind occurred in Birobidzhan.

Descriptions of the resettlement process and associated building usually lack any indication of an effective planning and organizing body. It seems that applicable training and competence were rare qualities among those charged to carry through the formidable and challenging undertaking of building the Jewish national unit. Ironically, *Birobidzhan Construction* (*Birobidzhanboy*), a 1932 poetic volume by Emmanuil Kazakevich, a 19-year-old Yiddish writer, carved a place in local history as the first book of literature published in Birobidzhan, rather than the name of an enterprise responsible for the Birobidzhan project. As a construction management, the Birobidzhan Construction appeared as late as 1935.

Ezekiel Groer, the second-in-command person in Agro-Joint, took to task the Moscow functionaries of OZET and KOMZET for making decisions "without preparatory work; without finding out where the people who should be settled on the land were; without finding out whether they were willing to settle on the land."[8] In July 1933, *Der Emes* mentioned the "decisive uncompromising struggle against the irresponsibility, carelessness and flightiness which have thus far ruled in Birobidzhan."[9] Soviet Ukrainian authors told, in their Birobidzhan travelogues, about the local managers' appalling incompetence and the rusting tractors, cars and other machinery sent by American sponsors.[10]

Ineptness and bungling coupled with extremely difficult climatic and logistic conditions led to a low retention rate of Jewish migrants. The job market of the time additionally complicated the process of resettlement: jobs or other opportunities, such as vocational or higher education, were often available in the growing large urban centers or even in a former shtetl. It was, ironically, one of the functions of the same KOMZET to support Jews with getting jobs in the rapidly developing industry. In 1928, Meir Alberton, a Yiddish writer who lived in the Ukrainian city of Dnipropetrovsk (now Dnipro), spent some time in Birobidzhan and then authored the book *Birobidzhan, Impression of a Journey* (1929), an account of the travails and heroism of the pioneer settlers. But later he wrote about the Jews who rebuilt their lives by becoming miners or factory workers in heavy industry. In the 1933 book *Day and Night* by the Moscow Yiddish writer Shmuel Persov, two groups of people left a shtetl in Belorussia, choosing different end-destinations for resettlement: one group went to

Birobidzhan, whereas the other group was dispatched to the coal and steel region in Ukraine. "Both trains will take them to different journey's ends, to different far destinations, but leading to the one and the same goal of building, creating and reconstructing."[11]

In the meantime, the resettlement to Birobidzhan made an incremental progress, especially as most of the arrivals rarely stayed long in the highly challenging environment.[12] The figures furnished by KOMZET evince a high percentage of leavers, but do not reflect the percentage of those leaving the region a few years later:[13]

Year	Arrived	Remained	Left (%)
1928	850	270	66
1929	1,200	840	33
1930	1,500	1,050	30
1931	3,250	2,600	20

Lev Baskin, a former teacher and a Communist veteran of the civil war in Ukraine who performed variegated duties of a representative of OZET, instructor, mechanic, organizer, boss and pedagogue, played a key role in deterring at least some ideologically charged pioneer settlers from taking flight.[14] The American Jewish socialist journalist Mendel Osherowitch described such young Jews, whom he observed in the Soviet Union, as zealots overwhelmed with a kind of religious "Hasidic exaltation." This state of mind made it possible to be ill fed, badly clothed and miserably lodged, but full of exhilarated enthusiasm for their participation in constructing a new way of life.[15]

A dozen of such "Hasidim"—or, rather, members of the Young Communist League, mainly students of the Jewish Agricultural College near the Belorussian capital of Minsk—formed the core of the commune ICOR, whose members arrived in Tikhonkaya on May 13, 1928, after travelling for over three weeks. In the Far East, they experienced enormous difficulties, including heavy physical exertion, dysentery, flooding and mismanagement, but did not desert the commune in the most problematic period of its existence. Some of them settled in Birobidzhan for good and married there. The first two children born in the commune were named Rosa and Vladlen, after Rosa Luxemburg and Vladimir Lenin. It turned out that the name ICOR had been chosen by the young men presciently—in the 1930s the commune received mainly immigrants from the United States who came lured by political or economic attraction, but often stayed there only briefly and then either returned home or, in rare cases, moved to other Soviet areas.[16]

Beginning from 1931, hundreds of foreigners arrived in Birobidzhan, notably from Lithuania, Argentina, the United States, France, Romania and Poland. Scores of people came from Palestine. As a rule, they were not complete foreigners, but rather people who had once emigrated from the territory of the Russian Empire. For instance, Luba Vasserman, who came from Palestine in 1934 and became known as a local Yiddish poet, was born and grew up in a Polish area of the former empire. Vasserman's husband, the Yiddish actor Moyshe Bengelsdorf, was also born in a Polish area of the empire and came to the Soviet Union from Argentina.

George Koval, the only Soviet citizen who later managed to get direct access to secret nuclear sites in the USA, came with his family to the Soviet Union in 1932 and settled in the ICOR commune. He was born in the United States in 1913 into a family of Russian Jewish immigrants, who got inspired with the Birobidzhan project. Koval went on to study in Moscow, where the intelligence service recruited him and sent him back to America. Drafted into the US army, he, following additional training, was assigned to work for the atom project and used his position to pass valuable information to Soviet nuclear specialists.[17]

Mary Leder, brought by her parents as a teenager from America to Birobidzhan in 1932, recalled about ICOR:

The gross inefficiency was compounded by deception and corruption. The Communist cell was a privileged caste. Supplies received for the entire section were divided unfairly, but any criticism of this practice was labeled a "remnant of bourgeois attitudes." The figures presented to the regional authorities in

Khabarovsk were falsified; accordingly, it took a long time to get to the bottom of what was really going on.

...My parents were miserable. Worst of all was their frustration at their inability to fight the petty and dishonest bureaucrats on the spot.... After nine months, they left Birobidzhan.[18]

Ben Zion Goldberg, wrote later, after turning from a supporter to a critic of Soviet policy towards Jews, that he used to detect greater enthusiasm for Birobidzhan in New York and Buenos Aires than in Moscow and Kyiv.[19] He also recalled his 1934 visit to ICOR, which he found in a very bad shape:

The rundown condition of the property, the drab, ramshackle buildings, the barren waste, their scrawny animals and fowls, were unmistakable signs of poverty and privation, of an unequal struggle with an unfriendly environment, of a defeat that they refused to accept.

We arrived toward evening, when the people were returning from the fields. The dirt of toil was on their hands and in the wrinkles of their faces, but there was no indication of happiness derived from communion with the soil. They looked more like Chinese coolies than Americans or people who had lived in America. Their old, threadbare American clothes showed through the openings of their short padded coats.[20]

Paul Novick, a journalist and later editor of the New York Yiddish Communist daily *Morgn-Frayhayt* (Morning-Freedom), admitted that the majority of the American re-settlers did not stay long in the Far East. He explained it by their unfitness for the strenuous work and compared them unfavorably with those who had come from Argentina and did not desert Birobidzhan.[21]

Goldberg saw a completely different picture in Valdgeim (or Valdheym, "Forest Home" in Yiddish), a village established less than ten miles from Tikhonkaya, which served as a showcase of the Far Eastern endeavor. "The settlement looked like a well-established, old-fashioned Russian peasant village: solidly built log cabins, each occupied by a single family—no doubling or trebling up as in other parts—with ample gardens well cared for. The people seemed hardy, well-fed folk."[22] Proximity to the central settlement was an important factor of success in a vast area lacking roads. A proper motorway less than eight miles long, was built between Birobidzhan and Valdgeim a year after Goldberg's visit. Leyb Reznik came to Valdgeim from Berdichev, which stood out in the Russian Empire as the town with a largest share (about 80 percent) of Jewish population, and soon earned the reputation of the best horticulturist in the area.[23]

It transpires that there were attempts to make the JAR populated not exclusively by Yiddish-speaking migrants from the Slavic republics, but to incentivize also Jews from Central Asia and the Caucasus to move to the Far East. However, such efforts had effectively come to naught.[24] Meanwhile, 1932 brought more Jews to the Far East. This could be a result of a better organization, the improved life conditions in the district and the severely worsening food situation in the European part of the country, particularly in Ukraine. Family clans that formed mutual help groups might have a better chance of success at settling and adapting in the new place.[25]

In 1932, the Birobidzhan District had 44,574 residents, including 5,125 Jews, or still less than a 12 percent share in the population. While the Russians (29,930) made up the majority of the local non-Jewish residents, there were also two other numerous ethnic groups: Koreans (4,175) and Ukrainians (2,375).[26] The population of the region reached 60,000 by 1933. Jews accounted for three-quarters of the increase and, as a result, made up about a quarter of the region's population. The percentage of Jews among the urban residents was higher—55. In all, about half of the Jewish settlers preferred to find a job and home in the growing central settlement, where their artisanal or other skills could find a better application.[27] A couple of years later, Kalinin criticized the ethnic divide between the heavily Jewish city of Birobidzhan and the predominantly Russian villages of the JAR.[28] Like in other areas of the Soviet Union, the agricultural sector of the JAR had two forms of organizations—collective farms (*kolkhozy*) and state farms (*sovkhozy*). The private sector had been effectively eliminated, though people were allowed, with a plethora of restrictions, to have a small private plot and to own a family house.

What kind of settlers did the authorities seek? An answer was formulated by the well-informed Yiddish writer David Bergelson, who after his emigration in 1921 lived mostly in Berlin, but since 1926 had been positioning himself as a Soviet writer. In 1932 he visited Birobidzhan for the first time and declared himself a passionate proponent of the project. In a letter, written in March 1933 from Copenhagen, where he had decamped with his family after Hitler's coming to power, the writer gave a rapturous description of the Far Eastern Jewish outpost:

> This socialist construction, which is part of the general socialist construction in the Soviet Union and therefore has the same great scale and great future, the completely new and extremely interesting human material, with these people's enthusiastic and heroic way of overcoming difficulties, the rapid development of a new multifaceted life on a multifaceted basis—everything was so unexpected and overwhelming for me that, as happens when one is destined to witness an event of great importance, I was simply unable immediately to start portraying the grandeur of what I could see all around me.[29]

To all appearances, Bergelson's visit to Birobidzhan became a salient factor in his fateful decision to resettle in the Soviet Union. His proclaimed fervor for the project fed expectations of him taking up residence in the new Jewish center, but he ultimately put down roots in far more habitable and attractive Moscow.[30] In his semi-fictional and semi-travelogue book *Birobidzhaners*, published in Moscow just before his return from emigration, Bergelson posited that the Far Eastern district was destined to be populated by a new kind of Jews, with values, aspirations and role models opposite to those of shtetl dwellers. The firstlings of the new Jewish socialist nation should forget the old world. The American Yiddish literary critic, Shmuel Niger, commented, insightfully, that in Bergelson's Birobidzhan characters one could not find traces of their past.[31] No place was left for specifically

Figure 2.1 David Bergelson, most probably in Birobidzhan. © Author's private collection.

Jewish ideological aspirations. According to Bergelson, people went to Birobidzhan in search of a better life, but "without any thoughts about a new epoch in Jewish history" and without any desire to become "ideologized Jews."[32] In other words, forgotten had to be the slogan "On to the Jewish land" as one that smacked of nationalism, an anathema for Soviet ideologues. Tellingly, a relation to the Zionist movement or to bourgeoisie disqualified applicants from registering for migration to Birobidzhan.[33]

Destitution—rather than a national-ideological drive—was considered the only justified motif for resettlement. Unqualified, jobless migrants were of a particular ideological importance for the task of remolding the bottom layer of Jewish society into productive members of the Soviet Jewish nation in making. To the consternation of Merezhin, many people with a skill, notably craftspeople, had chosen to go to Birobidzhan instead of doing what they were supposed to do: take a short cut to full membership in socialist society.[34] Significantly, by moving to Birobidzhan the disenfranchised Jews discarded their stigmatic societal status.[35]

Merezhin and his dogmatic ilk did not bother to factor in that such a complicated and massive construction site as Birobidzhan required expert work of trained people, including builders, carpenters, smiths, electricians, masons and mechanics. People of various trades, such as bakers, butchers, shoemakers and tailors, were also required to make the place habitable. Meanwhile, the trains brought not a few people, who were effectively unemployable for anything useful on a building site. Viktor Fink, a Russian-language Soviet writer, was astounded to see among the arrivals people having physical or mental disabilities, hardened criminals (they came from Minsk and Odessa), and prostitutes (from Bobruisk).[36] The migrants rarely had education beyond something basic. In fact, apart from physicians, teachers, construction engineers and agronomists, specialists with higher education would struggle to find a suitable job in the emerging rural and semi-urban economy.

In a contrast to the Jewish national districts in Ukraine and Crimea, which were entirely rural, with people living in villages ("colonies") and working predominantly in agriculture, in the Far East a new city would be built to serve as the local administrative, industrial and cultural center. Jewish functionaries and intellectuals cherished a dream about a metropolis with a modern infrastructure for work, education, leisure and culture. Clearly, some influential officials in the highest reaches of the Soviet leadership shared this vision of the future city.

Although the name of Birobidzhan continued to be widely used for denoting the entire region, in 1931 the official application of the toponym narrowed to only the administrative center of the district (until 1937 it had the status of an *urban-type settlement* rather than of a *town/city*), built on the site of and around Tikhonkaya. An urbanist project of the city was assigned to a team headed by Hannes Meyer, a Basel-born architect, who in 1930 emigrated to the Soviet Union. Previously, until his dismissal for Marxist sympathies, Meyer worked in Germany as director of the Bauhaus art school. The Bauhaus style, which aimed in particular to abolish the distinction between artist and craftsman, became an influential current in modernist architecture and partly defined, for instance, the urban landscape of Tel Aviv, with a zone declared a world heritage site by UNESCO.

Meyer's futurist project captivated the imagination of many people, including Bergelson. The future metropolis is depicted in *Birobidzhaners* as rivalling the great European capitals: the branches of the Bira will cut through the city just as the canals of the Spree permeate Berlin or as the Seine defines Paris. A cable railway, like those in the Swiss Alps, will run from the city to a *sopka*, as hills with a curved shape are called in that area. On the top there will be a sanatorium for workers and a colossal Lenin monument, equipped with lighting to make it visible at night on the other side of the border. The Jewish capital itself will be "a big, noisy city with a lot of factories on the outskirts, a completely socialist city in a classless society." The Birobidzhan trademark will be known all over the world. In New York and in Paris people will come to shops asking for a jar of Birobidzhan honey—a clear reference to the Biblical "land flowing with milk and honey."[37]

In the mid-1930s, Emmanuil Kazakevich authored a play, entitled *Milk and Honey*, about "a real homeland, a land of plenty, a land of milk and honey," which the Jews received from the Communist Party.[38] In the late 1920s, Kazakevich was one of the young Yiddish authors, then Kharkiv residents, who named themselves playfully Foygl-milkh (Bird's Milk, as a symbol of unachievable dreams). They did not stay in Kharkiv for long. Several years later, the Bird's Milk reunited for a while in Birobidzhan, moving there either directly from Kharkiv or after graduating from the Yiddish departments at pedagogical institutes in Moscow and Kyiv.[39] One of them, Buzi Miller, would become known as the most significant figure in the literary landscape of Birobidzhan and its permanent fixture. The majority of Yiddish writers, however, preferred, like Bergelson, taking literary pilgrimages to the Far East, while keeping their residence in a metropolis in the European part of the country.

Among the Yiddish writers flocking to visit Birobidzhan to marvel at its achievements was Hirsh Bloshtein, who settled in Soviet Ukraine in 1932 following his expulsion from Argentina for editing a left-wing Yiddish journal. He envisioned that by 1937 the city would "stretch its beautiful linear streets along the left bank of the Bira at the foot of the *sopka*. A young, beautiful, vibrant socialist city. A group of architects and expert engineers have been working over its plan." In the meantime, he did not fail to note that the town "had been built haphazardly." The writer got an impression of finding himself in "a large camp comprised of makeshift homes." However, neither the unattractive view of the randomly laid out town nor an incessant rain could dissuade Bloshtein from believing, or claiming to believe, that "the sun was rising above Birobidzhan, our great socialist sun, the sun of the working and free life."[40] In 1926, still in Argentina, Bloshtein penned a poem about many people's dream of becoming Soviet citizens and that they were like nomads who, exhausted by roaming in gloomy capitalist countries, reached out to the ever-sunny Soviet Union.[41]

The sun did not give rest to the writers' imagination. Bergelson in collaboration with Kazakevich declared that the sun shined in Birobidzhan three times more powerfully than the sun somewhere in Ukraine or Belorussia. "This sun, coupled with the sun of the Socialist Homeland, make the [Jewish] people healthy and strong."[42] Lord Dudley Marley, a British enthusiast of the Birobidzhan project who visited the area in 1935, wrote: "The climate is extremely healthy. In summer it is hot, but not too hot for comfort; in winter it is cold with snow but with a brilliant sunshine similar to conditions in Switzerland."[43] Even so, the sun never rose over a town designed by Meyer and his colleagues. The attitude to the foreign architect and his project was rapidly changing. There were also other hindering factors. Crucially, a large part of the area, where the new city was supposed to come up, had been commandeered for building a military compound.[44]

In the meantime, Birobidzhan grew into a muddy town of wooden houses hastily thrown together. Viktor Fink wrote that, on their arrival in Birobidzhan, both single settlers and families with children remained stuck for two or three months in barracks, living in conditions of extreme crowding, repulsive filth and permanent quarrels. Fink was not ready to categorize the wooden dwellings as "barracks for migrants" or even as a "transit prison." Rather, he characterized them as places for an accelerated course leading to admission at a mental asylum.[45] Ben Zion Goldberg stayed for some days in the autumn of 1934 in a clearing house for new arrivals to Birobidzhan and later shared his experience:

> None of the people I met there found the place better than they had expected. Most found it much worse. Some took the situation philosophically: Rome was not built in a day. Other, especially the practical wives, complained and protested. They had not been told the truth. They had not wanted to come in the first place. A frequent complaint was that although they had not expected to find a Garden of Eden, they had not expected such a hell, either.
>
> "What is the 'ḥell' of it?" I asked one disgruntled woman. She looked at me as though she had just noticed my presence, and must size me up to find out if I was acting the fool or had merely been born stupid. Hell meant a variety of things: the terribly crowded room at the clearing house, for instance, with no prospect of decent living quarters. They were told to be happy with what they had—the earlier pioneers had had to live in dugouts. Well, they had not come out here to live in dugouts. They had not had it that bad where they were. Hell meant joining a miserable collective farm, "compared to which the Belorussian peasant village was Paris," or going to work in a factory and earning more money, but finding nothing to buy with it, not even food, "plain food—say, a potato."[46]

Shifra Lifshitz, a political immigrant from Poland, who came to Birobidzhan to work as a teacher in 1934, initially lived in a small room with three beds. One bed was occupied by a middle-aged colleague, whose family planned to join him later. A young couple—a teacher and a college student girl—slept on another bed, a wider one. Later Lifshitz was fortunate to receive a room with an adjacent kitchen in a new wooden building. According to the building design, the room was intended to serve as a toilet for other flats on the floor but had been turned into a dwelling space.[47] As late as 1940, only 0.4 percent of all Birobidzhan dwellings had running water, 1.1 percent had sewage, and 5.9 percent had central heating.[48] On the other hand, a similar picture was in the majority of places of the former Pale.

Travelogues and memoirs are full of descriptions of the mire in the streets. Mary Leder's first impression of Birobidzhan stuck in her memory:

> I looked around me. There were signs of a recent heavy rainfall, but now the air was crisp and dry and the sun was shining. Beyond the wooden platform, the mud was knee-deep, as I could tell from the figures plodding through it.... It was late September 1931, and this was where our journey from California had ended, on a wooden platform in the middle of nowhere, on an island in a sea of mud.[49]

Bergelson recalled that in 1933 crossing a street presented a problem.[50] Osher Perelman, who came from Poland to see first-hand how Birobidzhan fared, noted a broken wooden sidewalk which added to discomforts of life.[51] Paul Novick wrote in his 1936 travel notes that one ought to walk carefully in the town, because the streets were not hard surfaced.[52] The first cobbled street appeared in Birobidzhan as late as 1937.[53]

In literature, the word "shtetl" frequently collocates with the adjective "muddy." Indeed, the center of the Jewish district took the shape of a shtetl rather than of a modern town. Producers' cooperatives, or *artels*, rather than industrial factories dominated the economy and consequently the job market in Birobidzhan. Particularly successful was the artel which specialized in producing the so-called Viennese chairs, made of bent wood. In 1929, several people from Malin, now a town in Zhitomir Region of Ukraine, had enough know-how to organize the production, using ash trees which grew in abundance in the area. A group of wheelwrights and wainwrights had formed an artel, named The Wheel of the Revolution.[54] Birobidzhan gradually developed as a regional center of light industry, including furniture manufacturing. This helped in particular to provide jobs to women, who made up more than a half of the Jewish arrivals, which reflected the demographic gender imbalance of the Soviet Jewish population.[55]

In the history of Birobidzhan, 1934 was a watershed year. On May 7, 1934, a decree raised the status of the area to that of the Jewish Autonomous Region (JAR) and thus created a shell for a Soviet Jewish nation-building project. The shell was almost empty: the eight thousand Jews who had settled there formed only 16 percent of the local population. Emmanuil Kazakevich portrayed the celebrations of May 7, 1934, as an interethnic event, which was welcomed also by the local Cossacks:

Later, during the rally in town,
An Amur Cossack comes out,
Strokes his beard,
Congratulates us
And dances a "Scissors" [traditional Jewish] dance with Jews.[56]

It was hardly a coincidence that the Soviet government's decree came against the backdrop of Hitler's achieving power in Germany. On May 10, 1934, *Izvestiia* (News), the second most important Soviet daily newspaper (*Pravda* was the most authoritative mouthpiece), published a front-page editorial, entitled "The Jewish Autonomous Region." It described the establishment of the JAR, a "region with a colossal future," as a "factor of colossal political importance." The editorial also mentioned the evil brought by fascism and racial theories. Earlier, in December 1933, the American press publicized Pyotr Smidovich's words that "Russia was able to render a shelter for prosecuted Jews from Germany" and welcomed them to take part "in the construction of the Autonomous Republic in Birobidzhan."[57]

The Soviet Union had been designed as a federation of constituent union republics with paraphernalia of independent states, including a full system of education in the titular nation's language. The Russian Soviet Federative Socialist Republic, the biggest and most dominant part of the union with Moscow doubling as the capital of Russia and the Soviet Union, and several other union republics contained smaller ethnic territories, republics or regions, with a lower, officially *autonomous*, status. Chronologically, the JAR was the last of the autonomous regions established in the Russian Republic before World War II. The Soviet constitution gave an autonomous region a vague right of *administrative* autonomy and an infrastructure for protecting ethno-national attributes, such as culture and language, from oblivion, which was less developed than in an autonomous republic. Like all other autonomous regions in Russia, the JAR was part of a *krai* (means "border" or "edge"), a region with a vast territory located along the geographical periphery of Russia. At the time of its establishment in 1934, the JAR belonged to the Far Eastern Krai and later, after a change in the territorial structure in 1938, to the Khabarovsk Krai.

The status of the territory determined greatly the nationwide status of the ethnic group, designated as the *titular* one even if it did not dominate numerically in that locality. While the token Far Eastern territory still had a substantially higher status than that of the Jewish rural districts in Ukraine and Crimea, the JAR played essentially a detrimental role in determining the entitlement that the Jews had in the Soviet pecking order. According to anthropologist Igor Krupnik, they "were condemned to a second-rate status in Soviet society, even without an anti-Semitic stance on the part of the regime." The national territorial categorization—the Birobidzhanization—did a disservice to the Jews by giving them a ranking along with other peoples of autonomous provinces.[58] Four years later it would "justify" the phasing out of virtually the entire Yiddish educational infrastructure outside the JAR. In somewhat of a short-lived policy reversal, Yiddish schools and publishing outlets would be opened in the territories, annexed by the Soviet Union along its western borders in the early phase of World War II, in 1939 and 1940. However, this did not change the situation in the "old" Soviet areas.

Crucially, Soviet Jews neither had, nor were permitted to have, any recognized voice of leadership to argue their case regarding the central authorities. As for the Birobidzhan officials, they, like their counterparts in other ethnic territories, were not supposed to have any pan-Soviet agenda to advocate before the Party and state leadership. For propaganda purposes, however, possession of a titular territory bureaucratically "normalized" Jews, making them match Stalin's definition of a nation as "a historically constituted, stable community of people, formed on the basis of common language, territory, economic life, and psychological make-up manifested in a common culture."[59] It also became a propagandist proof of "full solution of the Jewish problem" in the Soviet Union.

On May 28, 1934, Kalinin spoke to a group of Moscow workers and several Yiddish journalists. Also invited was Bergelson, who earlier that month repatriated to the Soviet Union and had already been admitted to the just-established Union of Soviet Writers, which enforced ideological conformity among the literary cadre. According to Kalinin, the foremost reason for the creation of the region was that the Jews were the only numerically significant—around three million—group without an autonomous unit which could serve as "the Soviet basis" for the Jews. He proclaimed that the existence of the region would make possible better development of Jewish culture. In the Soviet context it meant Yiddish culture, because Hebrew was deemed clerical and bourgeois, whereas Jewish culture in Russian was considered to be a latent form of nationalism.

Kalinin articulated his hope that in the next decade Birobidzhan would become the fulcrum of Jewish socialist culture and that even earlier, in five or six years, all Soviet Jews wherever they lived would associate themselves with Birobidzhan. In his vision of the future, the Birobidzhan Jewry would shed the traits of the Jews who lived or used to live in the shtetls of Poland, Lithuania, Belorussia and Ukraine.[60] The shtetl inhabitants continued to be viewed through the prism of unpleasant or comical stereotypes, which should be consigned to the history books en route to morphing the Jews into positive, actively contributing members of Soviet society.

It was believed that "autonomous region" was a temporary status on the way to proclaiming a Jewish autonomous republic. The word "republic" already figured in pronouncements of Soviet representatives.

The weekly newspaper of the Union of Soviet Writers, *Literaturnaia Gazeta* (Literary Newspaper), reproduced the speech made by the Tajik poet Abulkasim Lakhuti, who headed the Soviet delegation to the international Congress in Defense of Culture, conducted in Paris in June 1935. Lakhuti said, inter alia, that the Jews, a stateless, pariah people in the tsarist Russia, now had "their own republic—Birobidzhan, which is growing with a fantastic speed."[61] In 1936, speaking about the new constitution, Stalin explained that a union republic, or a constituent proto-state in the Soviet Union (such as Ukraine, Georgia, or Belorussia), had to have at least one million people of the titular nation living in this territory.[62] The criteria for an autonomous republic were less demanding; a hundred thousand was mentioned as the benchmark for being elevated to the status of such a second-tier republic. The number of Jews in the JAR, however, would never be even remotely close to this benchmark.

By 1934, the initial idea of encouraging migration to the Far East as a way to make Jews productive had almost vanished from the official narrative. Birobidzhan did not feature any more as a re-melting pot for the rejects of society. Ideologically, this objective had become incompatible with the claim that the Soviet Union had turned into a country of full employment. In addition, the Soviet decision makers had finally understood the obvious, that the region could not be developed without skilled people, able to work in the industrial and agricultural sectors of the local economy. In this context, Jacob Lestschinsky, a leading Jewish social scientist, who at that time lived in Poland, characterized the upswing in Birobidzhan-related activities as a bluff aimed at misleading thousands of people, including intellectuals of anti-Zionist, Yiddishist persuasions. Looking through his prism of Jewish activism, Lestschinsky could not find any economic or social rationale for this campaign, especially as productivization of the Jewish population clearly ceased to be the raison d'être for the JAR. Moreover, Lestschinsky fully agreed with the Soviet officialdom's silent admission that this cause had lost its practical reality.

Indeed, by the mid-1930s, each third Soviet Jew lived in one of the five biggest cities in the country: Moscow, Leningrad, Kharkiv, Kyiv and Odessa, where they had employment, often in prestigious occupational domains. In addition, the five Jewish national districts in the European part of the country had a population of around 200,000 Jews and the colonies could receive more settlers, partly as a replacement of those colonists who had moved to the cities. Furthermore, thanks to the full equality of Jews in Soviet society and the successful efforts to bring them into the new economic mainstream, the number of economically insecure people had declined from about one million in the early 1920s to 150–200,000, who, due to their age or other reasons, were unlikely to obtain the skills required for a gainful employment in Birobidzhan or elsewhere. Let alone that the relatively small number of people moving to Birobidzhan made it pointless to consider migration as a means of changing the structure of Soviet Jewry, who had been increasingly turning into "a nation of white-collar workers and doctors."[63]

The orientation towards recruiting qualified Jewish workers did not mean that the process of resettlement stopped pursuing the tasks of social engineering. Dimanshtein wrote in 1934 about a welcome development: the appearing of a new Birobidzhan generation—a kind of "cowboys of a socialist type," who did not carry "bad cultural habits."[64] Religion was one of such "habits," therefore synagogues categorically did not have a place in the emerging urban and rural landscape of the JAR. The region was built to house a militantly secular society, though among the migrants remained a small number of Jews who found meaning in traditional religious observance. David Khait, a Russian-language writer and journalist, recorded that by the mid-1930s the younger generation already knew very little about Jewish religious traditions. Young Birobidzhaners were bemused when a group of ethnically Slavic *subbotniks*, or Sabbatarians, settled in one of the villages of the JAR, but would not work on Saturday, because they were committed to living by Biblical law. Some Jewish jokers even offered the *subbotniks* their services as *shabes goyim*, or Gentiles hired to perform domestic chores forbidden to Jews on the Sabbath.[65] The Polish Jewish activist Perelman encountered, or chose to see, in Birobidzhan only several people, all of them *subbotniks*, who abjured pork.[66]

In their drive to transform the Jewish foodways, Bolsheviks reaped the fruit of secularization that had ripened before the 1917 revolution.

Back then an increasing number of young, modernized (and often radicalized) Jews rejected *kashrut*, and eating non-kosher often became a sort of an initiation ceremony during their gatherings.[67] In fin-de-siècle Kyiv and other Russian cities, numerous Jews, especially those on the higher rungs of the socioeconomic ladder, transgressed religious laws, including the ultimate taboo of eating pork.[68] In the late 1880s, radical groups among Eastern European Jewish immigrants in England and North America began to entertain themselves with food and dancing on the Day of Atonement, the most solemn and holy day of the Jewish year. The tradition of organizing "Yom Kippur balls" endured for a couple of decades.[69] Most Jewish cookbooks published in the United States before World War I contained non-kosher recipes and for the Jews who used them it was an ideological statement emphasizing their integration into modernity and American society.[70]

In the Soviet Union, de-kosherization was likewise rooted in ideology, which was of a more anti-traditionalist nature than the ideology of Reform Judaism. Disguised or undisguised, Jewish dishes ought to be freed from the restrictions of kashrut, because Jewish religious laws about the ritual suitability of food formed an obstacle to building a collective, ethnically variegated socialist society. For purely practical reasons, a nondenominational cuisine simplified catering in the army, children's and youth camps, factories and other public canteens. The army soldiers' religious or cultural differences did not impact what kind of food they would receive.[71] In addition, Jewish Communists, overzealous in their anti-religious campaigns, viewed kosher butchering "as ideologically repulsive, primarily because it created a source of income for the rabbis."[72]

A former member of the Tel Hai commune in Crimea, created by the Halutz (Pioneer) Zionist youth organization, reminisced later how their pig-breeders had been awarded the first prize at the all-Crimean agricultural exhibition, where their unusually larger and fecund Yorkshire pigs, presented to them by the JDC, became an object of general attention.[73] Later Tel Hai received the more appropriate name Oktyabr, or October, honoring the October 1917 revolution.[74] On November 1, 1928, the *Tribuna* wrote that a twenty-year-old graduate from a Jewish agricultural college was responsible for breeding pigs in Oktyabr, and that—reflecting the difficult Soviet-British relations of the time—he gave his pigs names of English lords. An agronomist Matvei Druianov published a number of Yiddish pamphlets, instructing how to work with pigs and rabbits (another non-kosher animal).

In the JAR pig breeding also symbolized a complete break with Jewish tradition. The Russian play *The Frontier Guard*, written by Vladimir Bill'-Belotserkovskii, contains the following discourse between a kidnapped Red Army Jewish soldier (Kogan) and his interrogator (Captain):

Captain   Jewish?

Kogan   Yes. A Jew of the Soviet land.

Captain   Why this emphasizing? Is the Jew of our land any worse?

Kogan   Maybe he is not worse, but he is worse off.

Captain   How about pork, do you eat it?

Kogan   Ask my father.

Captain   Why father?

Kogan   He is the best pig-breeder in Birobidzhan.[75]

Communists as well as other "politically conscientious" segments of the Jewish population were not supposed to burden themselves with following the "obscurantist" dietary rules of kosher cooking and eating. At the same time, non-kosherized Jewish food found appreciation as a valuable form of cultural expression. In February 1936, when Lazar Kaganovich, Stalin's Jewish lieutenant (at that time, People's Commissar, or Minister, of Railways), visited Birobidzhan, local housewives cooked for him *gefilte fish*, a staple of Jewish holiday dinners. In the event, the guest—who travelled in style, accompanied by a cook—did not touch the local food. The issue of gefilte fish emerged also during the visit of another Jewish guest—Polina Zhemchuzhina (Perl Karpovskaya). The name of her non-Jewish husband, Viacheslav Molotov, left a trace in the Molotov-Ribbentrop Pact (that effectively touched off World War II) and, rather irrelevantly, in the Molotov cocktail petrol bottle bomb. Zhemchuzhina, herself a high-ranking state functionary (at that time she headed a department at the Ministry of Food Industry), expressed her disappointment that this quintessential Jewish dish did not appear on the menu of the—apparently only—Birobidzhan restaurant.[76]

The ethnographers, who came to the JAR in 1937, faced problems trying to describe the national identity of local Jews through their customs, folklore and material artifacts. Their findings—certainly, partly at least, a reflection also of what the scholars set themselves the task of finding—were limited, above all, to ideological surrogates, such as photos of meetings discussing the new constitution and samples of Yiddish folksongs about Lenin and Stalin.[77] The scholars had found a much richer ethnographic material on local Koreans.

Summing up the first six years of the Birobidzhan endeavor, agronomist Druianov pointed to the following main problems: (1) in the spring and, partly, autumn months, lack of proper roads tended to cause a blockade of settlements distantly scattered over the region; (2) the harvest might be ruined by exceptionally wet weather, as it happened in 1928 and 1932 when heavy rains over summer brought flooding to part of the region; (3) bloodsucking insects, or *gnus*, remained an affliction, especially in a soggy summer; (4) the remoteness of the region made it difficult to bring essential materials for construction. And it remained no more than a hope to see more Jewish settlers coming to the Far East.[78]

CHAPTER 3
REPRESSION

Hitler's coming to power and unfavorable environment for Jews in some other countries, notably Poland, made the idea of resettling in Birobidzhan increasingly popular in Europe and even in the Americas. In 1934, the purportedly non-affiliated American Committee for the Settlement of Jews in Birobidjan (Ambijan) emerged effectively as a sister organization of the Communist-sponsored ICOR. In Britain, Lord Dudley Marley, deputy speaker of the House of Lords and chairman of the Committee for the Relief of Victims of German Fascism, graded Birobidzhan as "about the safest spot in the world." He also chaired the ORT Parliamentary Advisory Council that was established in Great Britain in 1930.[1]

In the autumn of 1934, a group of experts representing JDC and ORT, spent three weeks in the JAR. Judging by Joseph Rosen's report, they had concluded that the agricultural and industrial development of the region looked "quite feasible and possible" but required a tremendous investment. However, if the government was ready to absorb the heavy initial expenses and allocate its resources for solving the hardest and most critical tasks of road construction and land drainage and clearing, the opportunities for compact settlement of large numbers of Soviet and foreign Jews were greater in Birobidzhan than in Ukraine and Crimea.[2] James G. McDonald, an American diplomat who in 1933–35 served as League of Nations High Commissioner for Refugees Coming from Germany, noted in his diary on December 27, 1934: "Rosen has become almost an enthusiastic convert to Biro-Bidjan. He thinks it offers enormous possibilities for pioneer settlements—that is, for Jews from Poland and other Eastern parts of Europe, and only incidentally and for but a few German refugees."[3] In 1935, B'nai B'rith, an influential American Jewish conservative order, turned to consider the JAR as a site for migration of Polish Jews.[4]

In May 1936, Birobidzhan was visited by Adolf Held, president of the Amalgamated Bank, founded in New York in 1923 by the trade union Amalgamated Clothing Workers of America as an attempt to build elements of socialist economy inside a capitalist system. He travelled to Russia also—or even primarily—as a member of the American ORT's Board of Directors. In March 1936, the Soviet authorities allowed the ORT to send to Birobidzhan a group of 200 people, consisting mainly of ORT schools graduates from eastern Europe. The applicants were nationals of various countries, mostly Poland and Lithuania. The ORT began campaigning to raise money in support of emigration to the Soviet Jewish autonomy. In 1935, the ORT opened in Birobidzhan a sawmill, a veneer plant, a furniture factory, a woolen glove factory, two power plants, two training workshops and a number of truck gardens. All these employed over 500 people.[5]

In September 1936, *Forverts* published a series of Held's articles describing the situation in the JAR. He and his wife Lillian, one of the founders of the Milk and Egg League for New York's Tubercular Poor, travelled via Japan and Vladivostok. They arrived on a day off, which was neither Saturday nor Sunday. From 1931, the Soviet calendar was structured in accordance with six-day weeks—the sixth day of each new-style week was a day off. The streets were filled with people, prevailingly young people, dressed poorly, but clean in appearance. Linguistically, the dominant language in the town was Russian, though Yiddish, predominantly its Ukrainian dialect saturated with Russianisms ("two Yiddish words with eighteen Russian ones"), was likewise heard in the streets.[6]

In Birobidzhan, the Helds lived in one of the twenty rooms at the hotel section in the new railway station erected by prisoners of the Gulag, as the Soviet system of labor camps became known. In 1936, the Moscow *Pravda* reported the completion of the building of the station twice—on January 2 and October 21. In any case, it was almost ready in May, but prisoners still worked at the site. The construction engineer in charge of the project, also a prisoner, happened to be Jewish. One day Held spoke with him, in Yiddish. The prisoner-cum-overseer was very circumspect in his words and preferred to question

Held about the travails of American unemployed workers. In addition to the station, inmates were building a new movies theater. Held saw prisoners also on his way from Vladivostok to Birobidzhan. He was not allowed to visit any of the camps, situated outside the town, so he saw them only from outside and evidently heard perfidious stories about the living conditions of the inmates. Readers of his articles learned that the inmates were well fed, had educational programs for illiterate people and vocational training for people without qualifications. In Held's rosy picture, the camps had orchestras, theater troupes and other entertainments.[7]

Held had a long conversation with Joseph Liberberg, chairman of the Regional Executive Committee who came to Birobidzhan in 1934 from Kyiv, where he headed the Institute for Jewish Proletarian Culture. While himself a man of rather modest scholarly

Figure 3.1 Joseph Liberberg. © Courtesy of Iosif Brener.

accomplishment, Liberberg had achieved remarkable success in building up the largest Soviet scholarly body devoted to Jewish studies, and this apparently convinced him and the Moscow decision makers that he had a potential for succeeding also as the administrative head of the new region. It is hard to say that Liberberg really showed acumen for leading a project of gargantuan proportions, but he arguably was the most charismatic figure in Birobidzhan history. Years later Shifra Lifshitz remembered the strong impression he made on her: "He was an imposing, tall, handsome and strongly-built man. His inspiring and empowering speech made us ready to overcome all the difficulties associated with building [the region]."[8]

The top Soviet official in the JAR (though in the one-party Soviet system, Matvei Khavkin, the head of the regional Party committee, had more power than the head of the regional council) captivated the American guests, too. According to Lillian Held, "when one speaks with Liberberg, even the mud of Birobidzhan does not look so muddy." In this conversation Adolf Held characterized Americans' attitude to the Soviet Union as largely positive, which was particularly true for American Jews who remembered very well the role of the Bolsheviks' Red Army in protecting their brethren during the civil war. Hitler's coming to power made these sentiments more palpable. Held mentioned, though, that the destructive activities of American Communists angered people in the socialist labor movement.[9]

Held distilled his trip's impressions in two concluding articles. He saw as an exaggeration the widely circulated opinion that Jews had been resettled for acting as a shield in case of a military conflict in the Far East. At the end of the day, incomparably more Jews lived along the western borders of the Soviet Union, but this fact was not interpreted in the context of protecting the state borders. Various reasons were at play as people decided to move to Birobidzhan, come what may, but lack of job and social opportunities emerged as the most common push factor for migration. Held could not comment on the severity of the climate, because he visited the region in May, when the weather was agreeable. He did not notice any traces of religious life but attributed this aspect to the age structure of the population—the vast majority of the fifteen thousand Jews, including several hundred foreigners, were young and strikingly secular. The locals' living conditions in the houses, built without any kind of sanitation, looked appalling, but even such dwellings were in high demand. In sum, Held did not believe the area was able to receive more than five or ten thousand new settlers. Therefore, he reckoned, it was logical that the Soviet government had limited its quota for foreign immigrants.[10]

Nevertheless, during 1936, the Soviet propaganda machinery continued promoting Birobidzhan. Ambassador Troyanovsky's article praising the achievements of the JAR appeared in the American press.[11] In 1936, the talkie *Seekers of Happiness* was released, featuring Jews who came from abroad to settle in the JAR. In the United States, the film was shown under the title *A Great Promise* and faced ban (as "harmful propaganda") in some parts of the country.[12] The whole campaign, after all, was a futile waste of time. Less than 1,400 foreign individuals were permitted to move to the JAR between 1931 and 1936, and by the end of 1936, *Forverts* quoted Dr Rosen, who informed the newspaper that, "given the intricate international situation," Soviet authorities did not allow foreign Jews to move to the Far East.[13] Indeed, Soviet authorities closed access to the region for foreigners, whereas heretofore visitors and migrants used to come to the region from many countries.

On August 29, 1936, the Presidium of the Central Executive Committee adopted a decree about the further development of the JAR, paying most attention to measures aimed at bringing more people, especially Jews, to the region. The document also stated that the JAR was "turning into the center of Soviet national Jewish culture for the entire working Jewish population."[14] In December 1936 and January 1937, the Soviet Yiddish press announced that a Yiddish language conference would be convened in Birobidzhan on February 9, 1937, in commemoration of the "historic day" in 1936 on which Lazar Kaganovich had visited the JAR. The ostensible purpose of the conference was to solve various practical language-planning problems, which were dogging Yiddish journalists, teachers and scholars. In fact, more important was the conference's political agenda: its resolutions were intended to result in the establishment in Birobidzhan of academic and educational institutions, empowered to supervise the

Yiddish language and Yiddish culture in the Soviet Union. Some pro-Soviet Jewish circles abroad had signalled their readiness to recognize Birobidzhan in advance as the Mecca of modern secular Yiddish culture.[15]

In April 1937, several American Jewish newspapers informed their readers that the Soviet envoy Troyanovsky denied the rumors circulated about the Soviet government's decision to liquidate the Birobidzhan project. He pointed out that Article 22 of the new constitution made the JAR an integral part of the elaborate territorial patchwork shaping the Soviet Union.[16] Troyanovsky did not try to mislead the American public. The JAR, established under this name in May 1934, remained on the administrative map of the Soviet Union.

Nonetheless, the year 1937 bookended the period of its building as a territorial unit with a claimed potential to evolve into a significant center of Jewish life, perhaps even a Jewish republic. Scores of office holders in the Birobidzhan administration and local intellectuals vanished during the mass "purges" beginning from the end of 1936, but mainly in 1937, the year when the terror was at its height.[17] Ethnic operations were part of the purges. Hence the importance of the ethnic marker ("nationality") in the identity papers, which generally played paramount roles in Soviet society.

The most important document was the "internal passport," whereas the "foreign passport," needed for traveling abroad, was an abstruse abstraction in the country with hermetically sealed borders. The internal passport, on the other hand, was an indispensable element of of people's life. Introduced in December 1932, such identity documents had to be obtained by every urban dweller aged sixteen and older, but initially, and for over four decades to come, normally would not be issued to people living in villages, making it difficult for them to resettle without getting a special permission. The situation was different, however, in the Birobidzhan District and later in the JAR, because all adult urbanites and villagers living along the state's borders were required to have passports. The process—dubbed "passportization"—included issuing residence permits, known in Russian as *propiska*. A passport and a *propiska* (stamped in the passport) were essential for obtaining a job, entering into a civil marriage (which was the only state-recognized one), getting access to housing, and other bureaucratic necessities. By October 1934, upward of 23,000 residents of the JAR had received passports, whereas almost 2,000 for various reasons failed to pass the police check, which meant that they should move out from the security sensitive region. There is no information available about how many of them were Jewish.[18]

Passports contained various details about their holders, including "nationality" which, from 1938, could not be freely chosen. Rather, people would get documented ethnic markers of their parents. Applied to Jews, this universal rule meant that if both parents were Jewish, their children were categorized as Jewish by default. Children born to parents of different ethnicities had, at the age of sixteen, a binary choice between their mother's and father's backgrounds. This meant that even thoroughly acculturated people with two Jewish parents lacked a legal way to full bureaucratic assimilation. Religion did not find any reflection in the passport.

The passport and, generally, registration system found a sinister use during the repressions targeting specific ethnic groups. In September 1937, more than 4,500 Koreans were deported from the JAR, without even giving them a 24-hour notice to prepare for the journey. This was part of the first Soviet deportation of an ethnic group as a whole, undertaken in response to the July 1937 Japanese invasion of China. Korea had been annexed by Japan since 1910. In order to "prevent the infiltration of Japanese spies," the Koreans as well the Chinese, whose number was smaller, were to be evicted by early 1938 from all areas in the Soviet Far East and sent to Kazakhstan and Uzbekistan in Central Asia.[19]

The deportation took place against the backdrop of the mass repression unlashed to stave off perceived internal threats to the regime. In 1937 the wave of terror peaked and entered the historical vocabulary as the "Great Terror" or "Great Purge." In fact, the Soviet machinery of repression never stopped functioning. In 1933, scores of Birobidzhan residents were arrested as members of the "Peasant Labor Party," a fictional counter-revolutionary organization made up by the People's Commissariat for Internal Affairs (abbreviated NKVD).[20] In March 1935 a "counter-revolutionary group" was liquidated among the workers and master mechanics in Birobidzhan.[21] In 1935, the Birobidzhan NKVD officers reported liquidation of an anti-Semitic organization, which ostensibly had contacts with foreign agents and fulfilled the task of hindering the development of the Jewish autonomy. As a result, several people received prison sentences, whereas their purported leader was executed.[22]

Significantly, it is hard to detect in the campaign of terror any signs pointing to an anti-Jewish nature of the action. According to the historian Yuri Slezkine, "Jews were the only large Soviet nationality without its own "native" territory that was not targeted for a purge during the Great Terror."[23] In fact, following the establishment of the JAR Jews began to be treated as an ethnic group with a "native territory" and repressions there were rather devastating. More importantly, however, Jews did not have a "native territory" outside the Soviet Union (Palestine was not considered as such), which meant that they would not be collectively distrusted as being fully or partly loyal to a foreign state and therefore—potentially at least—disloyal to the Soviet

Figure 3.2 A 1938 pamphlet by Chaim Zhitlovsky, the leading American theorist of building a secular Yiddish-speaking Jewish nation. © ICOR, closed in 1946 and now out of copyright.

state. At the same time, Polish, Lithuanian, Latvian, German and Romanian Jews who had settled in the Soviet territory, often as political immigrants, stood a strong chance of being persecuted under suspicion of spying on behalf of foreign governments. In the JAR, as everywhere else, foreign immigrants had a tenuous chance of being spared from repression.

One more factor must be taken into account in order to understand why Jews were not targeted as a category: the Soviet regime prided itself on being the guarantor of Jewish safety and sought to show the difference between the treatment of Jews in the Soviet Union and in the west, especially in Nazi Germany. On November 30, 1936, *Pravda* reported Viacheslav Molotov's speech, in which he, then Chairman of the Council of People's Commissars (or effectively Prime Minister), quoted Stalin's comment circa 1931 on anti-Semitism. Now, five years after being formulated for an interview to the Jewish Telegraphic Agency and widely published abroad, Soviet citizens also learned that "anti-Semitism, like any form of racial chauvinism, is the most dangerous vestige of cannibalism." In the Soviet Union, however, "brotherly feelings for the Jewish people" defined the attitudes towards anti-Semites who could be severely punished, including the death penalty. The article "Jews in the USSR and in Fascist Germany" by the German-Jewish novelist Lion Feuchtwanger, published on March 20, 1937, in *Izvestiia*, brought home the contrast.

The "Great Terror" conducted by NKVD had engulfed all layers of society without exception, making it often hopelessly difficult to distinguish a consistent logic applied to choosing victims. Even so, the secret police markedly targeted more or less independently thinking men and women. People who demonstrated proactive thinking and initiative might seem less obedient to the regime. In the Birobidzhan saga, Joseph Liberberg was the most conspicuous person in this category. Moreover, he was a towering figure among the functionaries and activists dealing with various aspects of Soviet Jewish life.

Liberberg appeared in his new role of the chief administrator of the JAR a month after a Yiddish language conference, which he organized as director of the Institute for Jewish Proletarian Culture. The conference, convened in Kyiv on May 7–11, 1934, was the most representative forum in the history of Soviet Yiddish language planning. It is noteworthy that the opening day of the conference had been timed to coincide with the day on which the Soviet government declared that the Birobidzhan District had been raised to the status of a Region. Over one hundred delegates and numerous guests from twenty-five Russian, Ukrainian and Belorussian cities were addressed by Ukrainian Party and government officials.[24] Liberberg's ultimate idea was to build in the JAR an institute similar to the Kyiv one.[25]

As early as 1932, the institute took the initiative of setting up in Birobidzhan an academic outpost and sent there three graduate students and, a year later, a bibliographer. One of the graduate students, Ikhil Rabinovich, appointed to head the local teachers' college, was arrested and executed in 1937. The other two were also arrested, sent to labor camps, survived the incarceration and did not return to Birobidzhan. By the time of their arrests, Nathan Kopman was director of the Yiddish theater, while Benjamin Goldfain headed the education department of the JAR. Fate was somewhat kinder to Josef Eliovich, the bibliographer, who remained at liberty. In 1937 he began to work in Leningrad, at the Saltykov Shchedrin Library (now the National Library of Russia in St Petersburg), but his trace disappeared in 1942, when he had been drafted in the army.

The construction of a building for the Birobidzhan library began in 1936. It transpires, however, that initially the library was supposed to be at a different place, probably in the area envisaged in Hannes Meyer's project. Esther Shneiderman (later Rosenthal-Shneiderman), who worked at the Kyiv institute before moving to Birobidzhan and had unqualified admiration for Liberberg, reminisced half a century later that in the spring of 1936, despite being overloaded with pressing issues of daily life and work, he led a group of people to a snow-covered hill and told them: "Look, soon we'll start building here a library for Jewish books which will be the biggest in the entire world."[26]

Importantly, Liberberg was able to find common ground with intellectuals and specialists who by and large did not rush to settle in Birobidzhan. Khavkin, a shoemaker turned Party appointee, who was skeptical at best about Liberberg's academic and cultural projects, wrote nevertheless summing up the results of the first year of the JAR:

"now we feel a particularly acute shortage of intellectuals, culture workers, writers, artists, theatre workers and scholars."[27] Enthusiasts, often foreign immigrants, and graduates of higher and vocational schools sent to work in the region only partly filled the acute skills and expertise shortage. A host of them would be executed or sent to labor camps in 1937 and 1938.

In December 1936, *Der Emes* wrote that it was Kaganovich who had introduced the idea of convening a language conference scheduled to be held in Birobidzhan on February 9, 1937. (In August 1936, the Birobidzhan theater received the name of Kaganovich.) The preliminary conference program was dominated by speakers from Moscow, including Shimen Dimanshtein, chairman of OZET, Moyshe Litvakov, editor-in-chief of *Der Emes*, and David Bergelson, recognized as the most significant Soviet Yiddish prose writer. The agenda included also a paper on "the unification of dialects," presented by Chaim Holmshtok, who in 1935 moved from Minsk to Birobidzhan to head the Scholarly Commission of the Regional Executive Committee.[28] He stood out among the few local irrepressible enthusiasts who entertained the notion that the Birobidzhan Jewish population would in the not-too-distant future speak a uniform Yiddish language rather than pristine dialects. In May 1935 a special conference of Birobidzhan linguists, journalists and teachers had debated this issue.[29] In fact, the majority of the population was non-Jewish, and this restricted the use of Yiddish. Let alone that the younger generation felt more comfortable speaking Russian. Characteristically, the local theater, established in 1934, was obligated to form a Russian-language troupe.[30]

In the end, the debates and other preparations ended in naught. Shortly before the conference was due to have begun, an announcement appeared in the press about adjourning it until May. As it turned out, the conference never took place, above all because many of those who should have taken part began to be thrown in jail. Liberberg was the first victim. When Khavkin wrote in 1935 that among the re-settlers were "class-alien elements,"[31] he certainly could not envision that within one or two years both he and Liberberg would be categorized and treated as people posing a threat to the Soviet regime.

Liberberg was arrested in Moscow in August 1936 and executed in March 1937. He was deemed a leading figure in a Trotskyist conspiracy, a traitor, whose origins lay in the Labor Zionist party, "a turncoat who had misled the party authorities in the region all along, and who had until lately concealed his past." In May 1937 Khavkin was expelled from the Party. The journal *Tribuna* published a long article by Moyshe Litvakov, written in the usual Soviet style of invective, describing Khavkin and his fellows as "a repulsive pus canker" and accusing them of treachery, intrigue and especially of Trotskyism. This article was to no avail—either to *Tribuna* or to Litvakov: both were liquidated that same year.[32] Dimanshtein was executed in August 1938. Among the victims of the purges in 1937 and 1938 were Shmuel Weizmann, Abram Merezhin and numerous other people associated with the Birobidzhan project. Yankel Levin, the first Party chief in the Birobidzhan District and Khavkin's deputy by the time of his arrest, was executed as a "Japanese spy."

Like in other places, the Birobidzhan-based NKVD officers, some of them were Jewish, practiced various methods of torturing, including the so-called "conveyor": the victims were forced to run at a trot from one officer to the next. Each agent in turn cursed, threatened and questioned them, round and round, hour after hour, day after day. If they fell they were beaten, staggered to their feet and resumed the torment. This would continue until the tortured, mostly loyal Soviet people, had signed a self-incriminating confession of committing crimes which did not jibe with the reality of their lives. Joseph Baskin, a member of the Palestinian Communist Party who studied in Moscow and then settled in Birobidzhan, left a description of the horrific physical suffering he was subjected to by Birobidzhan NKVD officers.[33]

Mikhail Kattel, appointed to replace Liberberg, was removed in January 1937 and executed in September of that year. In June 1938, the new head of JAR, Miron Geller, was detained and sent to a labor camp. Khavkin was spared from execution, although a number of people had received capital punishment for their fabricated involvement in anti-Soviet activity under his leadership. Still, in January 1938 he was arrested and sent to a labor camp, where his shoemaking skills came to use and helped him survive the incarceration.[34] Unless it's an anecdote, his wife was grotesquely accused of trying to poison Kaganovich with gefilte fish of her cooking. Aron Ryskin, a tailor turned Party functionary, who replaced Khavkin, was removed in October 1937 and arrested in March 1938. Like Khavkin, he survived incarceration. The majority of Party functionaries and other office holders of the JAR were purged. Among the prosecuted were 286 of the 311 delegates who took part in the first Regional congress in 1934.[35] In 1937–1943, the Party organization of the JAR was led by Hirsh Sukharev, sent to Birobidzhan from Moscow, where he was in charge of the Party organization at his alma mater, the Moscow Chemistry Technological Institute. He represented the Soviet nurtured apparatchiks who considered to be fully loyal to Stalin.

In a telegram sent from Birobidzhan and published in *Literaturnaia Gazeta* on February 1, 1937, Bergelson wrote "it came as a relief to the entire Soviet people, to all the best citizens of our country to learn that the sword of justice had fallen on the necks of those who betrayed the homeland, socialism and toiling mankind." He was unharmed by the terror but remained in the category of ideologically somewhat questionable authors. Two years later, when six of his literary colleagues, including the poets Itsik Fefer and Peretz Markish, received state decorations, he did not become an "order-bearer" (*ordenonosets*), which was a highly honorary and remunerative status in society.

Although the 1937 conference was cancelled, the Kremlin began to treat Jews in accordance with the cut-and-dried pattern for peoples with national territories. Most significantly, after 1937 Yiddish institutions outside the JAR could be closed down "with a clear conscience," since the government typically did not sponsor similar institutions for the diasporas of other territorial peoples. As for those Jewish migrants who had settled in Birobidzhan, they were compelled to be satisfied with living in a small remote town or its surrounding villages, in "a factory for the assimilation of Jews" (as Buzi Miller put it later),[36] rather than in a Jewish cultural center. Not only an academic center was not established in Birobidzhan, but its model, the Kyiv institute, Liberberg's brainchild and creation, was closed in 1936 and replaced with a much smaller Bureau (*kabinet*) for Research on Jewish Literature, Language and Folklore.

It is telling that none of the more or less significant Yiddish writers had moved to Birobidzhan. Moreover, even those writers who appeared to put down roots there used any chance to move to Moscow or other places in the European part of the country. Little had come out from the attempt to create a literary milieu, which went hand in hand with the defunct broader plan of building a vibrant Jewish cultural center in the JAR. Among the leavers were Tevye Gen and Hersh Vaynroykh (Grigory Vinokur). Both worked on *Birobidzhaner Shtern* and later became known as prose writers. Hirsh Dobin, already a member of the Union of Soviet Writers, was arrested in 1938 as a "Japanese spy" and released in 1940 but did not return to Birobidzhan.

Kazakevich, Miller and their younger fellow litterateur Aron Vergelis, who grew up and revealed his poetic talent in the JAR, became members of the Soviet Writers Union on the same day in January 1940. Kazakevich and Vergelis were hailed as Birobidzhan authors, though they already lived in Moscow.[37] Kazakevich perspicaciously decamped to Moscow, realizing that the NKVD's "sword of justice" had raised over his head. The writing was on the wall: in November 1937, Kazakevich lost his status of a candidate member of the Party, because the three full Party members who had recommended him turned out to be "enemies of the people."[38] In September 1939, *Literaturnaia Gazeta* featured a short article, bylined A. V. (in all likelihood, Aron Vergelis), describing activities of Birobidzhan literati.[39] Joseph Rabin, dispatched from Moscow to head the Birobidzhan writers' organization, was not, and could not be, mentioned by A. V. Detained in 1937, Rabin would be released in 1943 and sent to fight with the Nazis.

Notwithstanding the ongoing wave of terror, the region celebrated the tenth anniversary since the start of resettlement to Birobidzhan. In the spring of 1938, the local authorities welcomed numerous guests, most notably representatives of OZET. This was the last chord in the history of both OZET and KOMZET, which would be liquidated in May of the same year. The remit of both agencies was narrowed in September 1936, when the government had reassigned the organization of resettlement to NKVD, putting the whole process under strict control procedures.[40] The military conflicts with Japan, notably the

Battle of Lake Khasan in July–August 1938, led to further tightening the control.[41]

During 1938, the Soviet Jewish cultural infrastructure which had hitherto acted as, to borrow the historian Terry Martin's definition, an "affirmative action empire," decreased. Gone were almost all Yiddish educational institutions. Gone was the Moscow daily *Der Emes*. Foreign Jewish organizations could not work in the USSR any more. In a sense, the JAR remained a remote, meager and poor oasis of Yiddish culture. In any case, local schools still had Yiddish classes.

On November 17, 1938, a decree "About arrests, prosecutor supervision, and course of investigation" praised the achievements of the NKVD in fighting with enemies of the people, but also reviled those who had ostensibly overstepped the line and thus became responsible for incarcerating innocent citizens. The decree marked an end to the Great Terror of 1937–1938. It did not mean that the machinery of repression was shut down. Still, the relative "liberalization" could misleadingly assure people that the bad time was over. Some even deceived themselves by believing they could get away with questioning or even criticizing government decisions.

Many people were very unhappy with the October 1940 decree which cancelled student scholarships and concurrently introduced (and kept until 1956) tuition fees for high schools, colleges and universities. Bendet Kopeliovich, a lecturer at the Birobidzhan Teachers' Training College and author of textbooks for Yiddish schools, made a misstep by giving his students an assignment to write a paper on the topic "With a scholarship and without it." A denouncement led to his arrest in December 1940. In March 1941 he was sentenced to eight years of forced labor and not long thereafter died in the Gulag.[42]

Liberberg's and his associates' cherished dream about building a world important center of Yiddish culture did not come true. The majority of the visionaries perished during the purges. The JAR would never regain the white-hot enthusiasm and the rather strong intellectual capacity of the group assembled in Birobidzhan. The town continued to grow but remained a deeply provincial place like many others in the country.

CHAPTER 4
THE 1940s: NEW HOPE

The year 1938 is often considered to signify the end of organized resettlement of Jews to the JAR and the five Jewish districts in the European part of the country. In fact, the next year saw a seemingly little successful attempt to incentivize Jews, most notably Jewish collective farmers from other areas of the country, to move to the JAR. In August 1939, *Izvestiia* proudly reported that the country had 515 Jewish collective farms.[1] Only eighteen of them were in the JAR, which had in total sixty-four collective farms. A pamphlet, *What a Re-settler Must Know about the Jewish Autonomous Region*, published in Yiddish in 10,000 copies, contended that many of the Jewish farms in the European part of the country suffered from lack of land. As an example, it was mentioned the Jewish collective farm Bolshevik, situated near Grozny, the capital of the Chechen-Ingush Republic. Its members—Mountain Jews who spoke a version of the Tat language related to Persian (so they could not read the pamphlet)—were more involved in producing candles than in agricultural activity.[2]

On January 29 and February 28, 1940, *Pravda* published short articles under the title "Re-settlers to Birobidzhan," reporting that hundreds of peasants were moving to collective farms of the JAR from land-hungry areas of Russia and Ukraine. In fact, little came out of this. In 1940, 153 families joined the Jewish collective farms of the JAR and 32 (apparently non-Jewish) families moved to the so-called Red Army collective farms.[3] In the 1930s, demobilized soldiers were actively recruited to settle in the Far East as an alternative to the Cossacks who had performed similar functions during the tsarist era.[4] Around the same time, Germany signalled an initiative to transfer tens or even hundreds of thousands of German and Polish Jews to the Soviet Union, but the Soviet side turned down the offer.[5]

Against this backdrop, Hirsh Sukharev wrote to Georgy Malenkov, a Party official close to Stalin, about the urgent necessity to stop the continuing decline of the local Jewish contingent. In 1937 the number of Jewish residents reached a peak of 20,000, but two years later was under 18,000, making up only about 16 percent of the region's population. To illustrate his argument, the Party chief of the JAR mentioned that local Yiddish schools struggled to fill the classes and that *Birobidzhaner Shtern* had a meager circulation of one thousand copies. Sukharev suggested to start relocating to the region tens of thousands of Jews from the Polish territories, now western areas of Ukraine and Belorussia, annexed by the Soviet Union in the starting phase of World War II.[6]

The entire existing infrastructure of the JAR needed to be built up to meet the new demands. The regional authorities suggested that the government of the Russian Republic should approve the expansion of the city of Birobidzhan to accommodate an additional population. On March 9, 1941, *Izvestiia* published an abridged version of Sukharev's speech delivered to the congress of the Supreme Soviet (parliament) of the USSR. While ritually paying encomium to Stalin and reporting achievements of the region, he also complained that the government of the Russian Republic and the administration of the Khabarovsk Krai paid little attention to the needs of the JAR. A commission of the Republic's government spent a month in the region, but the government still did not consider its report. A project aimed at developing the city of Birobidzhan stuck in the red tape bureaucracy of the government for three years.

Probably as a reaction to the criticism, on May 5, 1941, the Khabarovsk Krai Party Committee and the Executive Committee adopted a joint resolution, "On Measures for Economic and Cultural Construction in the Jewish Autonomous Region," which may be inferred as an intent to prepare a ground for mass resettlement.[7] On the other hand, it remains unclear if Stalin and his advisors would even contemplate giving a green light to a mass relocation of essentially foreigners to an area that was at risk of turning into a theater of war with Japan. In any case, the plan—which in the case of its realization could have saved many a life and greatly reinforced the JAR—did not have a chance to be implemented after the German attack on the Soviet Union on June 22, 1941. That date marked the beginning of the Great Patriotic War, as the bloodiest phase of World War II was termed in the Soviet Union.

In 1941–1945, over 12,000 residents of the JAR were drafted into the war, about a half of them were killed, died of wounds or went missing. In all, the population of the region had thinned during the war.[8] Due to the remoteness of the Far East and the threat of a military conflict with Japan, only a trickle of the stream of evacuees from the war-affected areas had reached the JAR, whereas the Jewish population had increased manifold in many cities in other eastern areas of the USSR. None of the several professional Yiddish theater troupes, nor the Kyiv Bureau for Research on Jewish Literature, Language and Folklore, which endured after evacuation from the war zones, had been sent to Birobidzhan. The surviving Yiddish writers and journalists either served in the army or found a refuge in various places, but again not in Birobidzhan.

Despite the fact that Solomon Mikhoels, director of the Moscow State Yiddish Theater, emerged as the towering figure in the Soviet Jewish cultural—and, to an extent, political—landscape of the wartime, Yiddish writers, rather than theater people or scholars, played the most visible role in the 1940s. They became particularly prominent as central figures in the Mikhoels-chaired Jewish Anti-Fascist Committee (JAFC), the only nationally and internationally conspicuous Soviet Jewish body of the 1940s. The JAFC's leaders retrospectively associated the beginning of its activity with the carefully stage-managed rally, convened on August 24, 1941, at Gorky Park, Moscow's popular outdoor space. Broadcast over Soviet radio, the rally was recorded as a documentary for domestic and international release. A similar meeting took place in Birobidzhan, at which the "workers of the Jewish Autonomous Region" joined their voices to "the appeal that has come from Moscow."[9] It seems that the agitprop officials responsible for organizing the Moscow rally did it without even thinking about establishing any committee whatsoever. However, the enthusiastic response among Jews in the United States and other countries to the rally's appeal—to unify for fighting against the Nazis—opened the door to institutionalization of the JAFC in February 1942.

The name, Jewish Anti-Fascist Committee, sounded deceptively like the re-emergence of an element of Jewish civil society. The Soviets had a long track record of setting up organizations with misleading facades and using them for interaction with foreign counterparts. The JAFC had four sister wartime propaganda outfits—the All-Slavic Anti-Fascist Committee, and the Anti-Fascist Committees of Soviet Women, Youth, and Scientists—which all belonged to the Soviet Information Bureau (Sovinformburo), set up at the People's Commissariat (Ministry) for Foreign Affairs on the third day of the war, June 24, 1941. No one expected people to volunteer for membership in the anti-fascist committees. Rather, officials in the Party and state apparatus carefully selected and vetted the salaried staff and the membership of hand-picked authors (mainly, but not only, Yiddish), officers and generals, actors, artists, physicians, scholars, and representatives of the JAR, including Alexander Bakhmutsky, the Party chief of the region who was appointed to this position in April 1943, and Mikhail Zilbershtein, chairman of the Regional Executive Committee, appointed a year later.

As the time went by, however, the merely propaganda bureau increasingly turned into a surrogate central Jewish organization, though it had a little leeway for consequential decisions and actions. Members of the committee found themselves juggling their frequently conflicting roles of Soviet patriotic propagandists and Jewish activists. Some of them called on broadening the scope of their "extramural" activities, responding to the requests for help concerning various problems and grievances, which dogged Jews who survived the occupation or, more often, returned from evacuation.

In 1943, Solomon Mikhoels and Itsik Fefer where selected to represent the JAFC on a high-profile propaganda tour in the United States, making shorter appearances in Canada, Mexico and England. In their public addresses, the Soviet delegates did not forget to hail the achievements of the JAR. Mikhoels stressed that its establishment was significant:

> not only because it solves the problems of the Jews who live in Birobidjan, [but also] because it solves the problems of the Jews

of the entire country. The elements of statehood now enter into the picture of Jewish life in the USSR. We Jews have now become a people with equal rights, a people with state rights, not only a people with the equal rights of Soviet citizenship.

Fefer read his poem "Wedding in Birobidzhan" which described the Far Eastern region as a land of plenty:

Long and groaning tables, decked in linen white and pure.
Juicy ducks from Valdheym and fish from the Amur
It wasn't just the ducklings and surely not the goose.
It really was the Biro people—the Birobidzhan Jews.

Poultry stuffed to bursting point, livers chopped in fat,
The tables staggered with the load of everything they had.
Cakes well-soaked in honey—strudel with "kishmish"—
To say nothing of that truly Jewish and—gefilte fish.[10]

In 1944, Marc Chagall illustrated a wedding scene, which he based on Fefer's poem. Chagall also designed the cover for Fefer's poetic collection published in New York in 1943.

In the meantime, Mikhoels and Fefer had learned that the JDC preferred to sponsor a post-war resettlement of Jews to Crimea rather than Birobidzhan. In the event, the leaders of the JAFC too were ready to write off Birobidzhan as a complete failure and to return to Crimea as the main site for Soviet Jewish nation-building. Whether they realized this or not, they walked on thin ice, suggesting that the vaunted state-initiated venture should be buried in favor of a project based on an initiative of Soviet and foreign Jewish activists. The trip, which was dramatically consequential for the committee institutionally and for its members and associates personally, had charged Mikhoels and Fefer with confidence that they could make history and act beyond the remit of a merely propaganda outfit.

In a letter, written in February 1944, the JAFC asked the Soviet leadership to consider the proposal of choosing Crimea as a place of ingathering for the surviving Jews, scattered all over the country, and building there a Jewish republic. In the event, the letter did not achieve the desired result and would be later used as an incriminating document, pointing to an alleged anti-Soviet plot, aimed at creating a conduit for imperialist penetration.[11] In the meantime, the Birobidzhan drive was partly and only briefly revived after the war, despite Stalin's skepticism about the prospects of the region. During the Yalta Conference in February 1945, convened to discuss the post-war reorganization of Germany and Europe, he said:

> the Jewish problem was a very difficult one—that they [i.e., the Soviet government] had tried to establish a national home for the Jews in Birobidzhan but that they had only stayed there two or three years and then scattered to other cities. He said the Jews were natural traders but much had been accomplished by putting small groups in some agricultural areas.[12]

In December 1945, the Party and administrative heads of the JAR, who presumably knew about the "Crimean letter," made an audacious move by writing to Stalin to suggest that the Jewish autonomy be upgraded to the level of a republic. They were presumably encouraged by a good sign received from Moscow in 1944: a telegram which came from Stalin personally, the year of the tenth anniversary of the JAR. The telegram did not mention the anniversary of the region, but was addressed to the Yiddish theater, also established in 1934. Stalin thanked the theater collective for collecting money to meet the needs of children of soldiers at the front. Stalin's "greeting" coincided with the renewal of publication of *Birobidzhaner Shtern* on August 31, 1944 (it was interrupted in the war years) and was immediately published there.[13]

Although the Kremlin was not forthcoming about creating a Jewish republic, in 1946 and 1947 the JAR was reinforced with specialists, equipment and funds. On January 26, 1946 the government of the Russian Republic adopted a decree, "On Measures to Strengthen the Further Development of the Economy of the Jewish Autonomous Region," which was a day later supplemented by a decree of the government of the USSR on the construction in the JAR of a number of large industrial enterprises and thus providing jobs for the re-settlers.

Some attempts were made to reinforce the role of Yiddish in the region. Although most of the plans came to nothing, *Birobidzhaner Shtern*, hitherto a weekly, began to come out three times a week and there was established a new Yiddish literary almanac entitled *Birobidzhan*. The majority of the adult Jewish dwellers of the region were fluent Yiddish speakers, but only a relatively small proportion of them could, or wanted to, read in Yiddish. Still, for some of them *Birobidzhaner Shtern* remained the only newspaper they read.[14] The journal *USSR*, published by the Soviet Embassy in the USA, included in its May 1947 issue an article, "The Birobidjan Region," by Grigory Zhitz, editor of *Eynikayt* (Unity), the newspaper organ of the JARC. Zhitz stated that the JAR faced "inexhaustible opportunities for economic and cultural progress" and "with the help of the Soviet Government and the fraternal Russian people, the Jews of the USSR are transforming the Jewish Autonomous Region into one of the most advanced regions of the country."

The government sponsored a Birobidzhan-directed migration of the Jewish flotsam of the war. A decree provided means, in particular, for the resettling of hundreds of pre-war residents of Jewish agricultural colonies in Crimea and Ukraine. In addition, the government instructed the recruitment by the JAR of fifty teachers and twenty physicians, all of them Jewish. Representatives of the JAR toured the towns of Ukraine and Belorussia as part of the recruitment drive. The majority of new migrants had come home from evacuation somewhere in the eastern areas of the country and then, a couple of years later, moved once again eastwards to the JAR. There could be various reasons for doing this, including a desire to live in a Jewish cultural environment and at a distance from the mass graves of the Holocaust. In a letter published in *Birobidzhanskaia Zvezda*, one of the re-settlers wrote that his wife and two children had died during the war and that he hoped to heal his loneliness in Birobidzhan.[15] All in all, in 1947–1949, twelve specially assigned trains brought about 6,500 people. Jews came also in smaller groups and individually. All in all, the in-migration over this two-year period apparently totalled about 10,000 persons.

At the same time, upwards of eight thousand demobilized non-Jewish soldiers and officers were incentivized to settle in the region.[16] The practice of populating the Far Eastern villages with demobilized soldiers originated in the 1930s, particularly for replacing the expelled Korean farmers. Like in the pre-war period, many Jews and non-Jews soon moved from the region if they could not find satisfying jobs and accommodation. In all, it seems that the resettlement campaign brought the total of Jews in the region to about 17,000, or the same number as a decade earlier.[17]

In May 1946, the 30th anniversary of Sholem Aleichem's death was widely marked in the Soviet Union. The classic Yiddish writer had a place of honor in the Soviet literary and general cultural canon. Ben Zion Goldberg, vice-president of Ambijan, who was at that time in the country, said at a jubilee gala in Moscow that should Sholem Aleichem, his father-in-law, be alive, he would have felt at home only in one country—the Soviet Union.[18] A few days earlier, the Sholem Aleichem Street appeared in Birobidzhan. The local functionaries, who hoped to revive the campaign of building a strong Jewish polity in the region, decided that it was appropriate to have a "Jewish" thoroughfare. Sholem Aleichem already had a presence in the city: the local library was named after him in 1940, the year of its opening. Thanks to the extraordinary status of Sholem Aleichem in the canon of Soviet culture, the library and the street could keep their names even during the coming purges.

Der Nister (Pinkhas Kahanovitsh), one of the foremost Soviet Yiddish writers, travelled with a train of re-settlers and penned an enthusiastic documentary story "Together with Re-settlers to Birobidzhan" about the post-Holocaust "ingathering of the exiles."[19] In 1947 and 1948, the Moscow Jewish publishing house Der Emes produced Yiddish books, fully or partly dedicated to Birobidzhan. While Der Nister returned to Moscow, several Yiddish writers moved to Birobidzhan. The veteran proletarian Yiddish writer Joseph Rabin, who led the Birobidzhan writers' organization from 1936 and until his arrest in 1937, was not among them, although he survived the Gulag and then the frontline of the war. His first post-war book, *We Live* (1948), contains a story called "Trains are Coming." Its protagonist, Nyome Lybitsh, had managed to escape the ghetto in Belorussia, joined the army, and by the end of the hostilities, at a hospital, where he underwent treatment for a wound, opted to go to the JAR rather than to his home town devastated by the war. He arrived in Birobidzhan with several other demobilized Jewish soldiers and immediately felt happy there:

> Nyome is going slow to the park. He wants to see people, speak with somebody, and tell somebody that his heart is full of joy. [...] He sees people around himself—old and young ones, children. He is thinking about looking around, approaching one of them, and telling him at least a couple of words. At the end of the day, it is not important who this person is. All of them are his kith and kin.[20]

Like in other parts of the country, the Jews who had settled in the JAR were predominantly secular and devoted Soviet patriots. In his analyses of the social and demographic transformation of Soviet Jewry, Israeli historian Mordechai Altshuler came to the (somewhat exaggerated) conclusion that, following the loss of "a relatively higher proportion of elderly people, women, children, Yiddish-speakers, the less-educated, and those less integrated into the higher strata of Soviet society," "Soviet Jewry after the war had little cultural or social resemblance to what it had been only a few short years before."[21] In any case, the majority of them began favoring Soviet holidays, such as the New Year, May First International Worker Day and the October revolution anniversaries, over ones associated with the Jewish traditions.

For all that there were local Jews who had not abandoned their religious beliefs. During the war and shortly after the war, the believers had more latitude, because the Soviet stance on religion had become somewhat milder. Characteristically, in 1943 the Moscow Choral Synagogue had been finally allowed to get a new chief rabbi, Shloyme Shlifer, who became a member of the Jewish Anti-Fascist Committee (the previous rabbi had been executed in 1938). It was against this backdrop that the Birobidzhan religious community was registered on December 15, 1946—for the first time in the history of the JAR. Initially, it had a membership of three hundred. It figured in the registration documents that the community had unofficially existed since 1934. The synagogue was opened in March 1947. Nonregistered religious groups existed in several other places of the JAR. Some assistance came from the Jewish community of the Siberian city of Irkutsk, where Jews began to settle as early as the 1820s.

According to Israeli historian Ber Kotlerman, the first years of the community's activities represented a unique case of a linkage between a synagogue and the local establishment. Several members of the community were parents of regional and city functionaries. In addition to granting a building for the synagogue, the authorities passed an ordinance allocating a section of the local cemetery to the Jewish community. It was openly discussed whether Jewish calendars might be issued and a kosher meat market opened. Ultimately, when a harsher wind began to blow from Moscow in 1948, the Birobidzhan authorities found these development disturbing and undertook propaganda and administrative measures to stigmatize and marginalize the congregants. Predictably this led to a decline of synagogue attendance.[22]

The vast majority of the so-called "Birobidzhan generation" had nothing to do with religion. The notion itself of a "Birobidzhan generation," the "cowboys of a socialist type" as Dimanshtein described them in the 1930s, appeared in the titles of Aron Vergelis's collection of poems and Shmuel Gordon's story published in his book *Birobidzhaners from Way Back*. According to the latter, "It is the generation that already does not know any other home apart from Birobidzhan. For these young people, everything here is natural—the taiga, the *sopkas*, the great and hard work that they are doing. Unnatural sound to them stories about the former life in the shtetl." Still, a perceptive writer of predominantly documentary prose, Gordon recognized some outward visible signs revealing that a distinct cultural identity nevertheless survived in the JAR. The peace on the eve of the day off, now Sunday rather than Saturday, reminded him the shtetls of Ukraine and Belorussia:

Around the houses, smartly dressed women were sitting, cracking dried filberts, and waiting when their husbands and children would return from the bathhouse. In the heat of the day—the sunset just started—these women were sitting muffled in silk shawls, in which they perhaps once paid visits on Sabbath or holidays. From the open doors and windows one could savour a strong scent of gefilte fish and carrot-tsimes. The houses and gardens looked festive.

This revelation angered the Birobidzhan leadership, and in March 1948 they hurried to report to the Central Committee that Gordon had shown sympathy to "old national and religious traditions."[23] Bakhmutsky and other top officials were on the edge, falling over themselves to demonstrate their vigilance. They were aware that dark clouds had been gathering over them. Trouble began soon after a visit by a fact-finding commission, headed by Dmitrii Polianskii, chair of the Russian Republic's government a decade later. Back then he came as a functionary at the Central Committee's Directorate of Personnel. In February 1948, Polianskii reported that the JAR was rife with ideological, political and economic errors, abuses and corruption. He also noted that while Jews comprised only around fifteen percent of the total population of the region, they nevertheless dominated among the local top Party officials.[24]

Meanwhile, the state-sponsored resettlement of Jews to the JAR was undercut by the authorities' fear and dread of Jewish nationalism, especially after the establishment of the State of Israel in May 1948. "The fifth point," widely used as a metonym for "Jewish," in the internal passports began to play often a key or even fateful role in various aspects of life, including choosing and gaining access to professions, some of which had become increasingly almost entirely out of reach to Jews. (In fact, the folklore around "the fifth point"—"invalid of the fifth point," etc.—stems from the ordinal number of the entry not in the passports, but in standard forms used by personnel departments.) This treatment of Jews as an outgroup did not appear out of nowhere. Gennadii Kostyrchenko, an insightful student of Soviet Jewish history, traces the origin of the policy of discriminating Jews to the Directorate of Personnel, established at the Central Committee of the Communist Party in 1939. The second half of 1942 and especially 1943 saw numerous dismissals of Jews from leading positions in the domains of culture and propaganda.[25] In the sarcastic words of the film director Mikhail Romm, "Until the year 1943, as we know, we had no anti-Semitism. . . . Somehow, we managed without."[26]

In the wake of the establishment of Israel in May 1948 (albeit this was not the only motive for the action), an increasing number of Jews, including cultural figures, faced suspicion of harboring and propagating nationalist sentiment, loyalty to Zionism and admiration for Western values. In 1948–1953, the ongoing repressions against various groups of the population targeted specifically also Jewish intelligentsia, professionals, religious activists and functionaries all over the country. In November 1948, the authorities liquidated the JAFC and began dismantling the entire remaining infrastructure of Jewish cultural life and arrested scores of writers, journalists, scholars and actors. Thirteen members and employees of the JAFC were accused of anti-Soviet conspiracy and executed on August 12, 1952. Earlier, in January 1948, or before the establishment of Israel, a staged road accident cut short Mikhoels's life. This was followed by a state funeral. A memorial service was also held in Birobidzhan and for several days the local press was filled with items about Mikhoels. At the beginning of February, the Regional Executive Committee took the initiative of rebranding the Workers' Club of the Industrial Cooperative Society as the Mikhoels House of Culture.[27]

In the last months of Stalin's life (he died in March 1953), scores of Jewish physicians, along with other medical professionals, were scurrilously accused of anti-Soviet plotting. Five years after his death and official eulogies, Mikhoels was among the names identified in the purported conspiracy. The ensuing smear campaign in the media found an approving or even gratifying response on behalf of parts of the population. During the rallies and private conversations, in the heat of the "doctors' plot," people in various corners of the country were talking openly about their desire to see the Jews being evicted one and all to Birobidzhan or Israel. Some even expressed their displeasure that the Germans failed to finish them all off during the war.

The situation in Birobidzhan aggravated dramatically in 1949 and 1950, when the leading Party and administrative figures of the region, many local intellectuals and managers were accused of nationalism and various types of sedition. In addition, there was a murky affair with an orphanage or, to be precise, an idea of establishing a Jewish orphanage. A considerable amount of goods, equipment and building material had been bought or collected thanks to a large-scale campaign organized in the United States. It seems, however, that the campaign turned out to be futile, because much of what had reached Birobidzhan ended up being mismanaged, diverted for other purposes or even misappropriated.[28] In 1948, a CIA "source" in Birobidzhan reported that US-made goods, primarily clothing, appeared in local state stores. The sale prices of the items were very low. To all appearances, the goods had been received as part of the aid collected by American Jewish organizations.[29]

We can only guess if Bakhmutsky, a relatively young (born in 1911), ambitious man, who grew up in a Russian-speaking family and did not know Yiddish, had miscalculated badly and aggravated his position by trying to elevate the status of the Far Eastern Jewish territorial unit—from a region to a republic. It is quite possible, though, that he and his "associates" simply happened to be at the wrong time and place and would have been arrested even if they kept a low profile. In any case, Bakhmutsky was given the death sentence which was commuted to 25 years of forced labor imprisonment. Mikhail Zilbershtein and Mikhail Levitin, who replaced the former as chairman of the Regional Executive Committee, were sentenced to the same term of incarceration. (Bakhmutsky and Zilbershtein were released and acquitted of the charges in the mid-1950s, whereas Levitin was murdered in prison by criminals.) The Kremlin obligated the new regional leadership to break off relations with all non-Soviet supporters. The JAR had been made off limits to foreign visitors.

Judging by the minutes of a meeting of Communists working for *Birobidzhaner Shtern*—whose leading authors had been arrested in the last spate of Stalinist purges—the climate in the collective was tense. One of the journalists, Max Riant (who was not arrested), recalled that they were wary of speaking Yiddish even in the office, let alone in the street. In general, they "had the feeling of being trapped and, to be honest, feared that the authorities would close the newspaper." Indeed, there was an attempt to do so. Pavel Simonov, a non-Jewish functionary sent from Moscow in 1949 to replace Bakhmutsky as the Party boss of the JAR, suggested turning the newspaper into a weekly Yiddish supplement to its Russian-language sister publication. However, Smirnov's plan did not get the go-ahead by the central Party apparatus. The token autonomy had to have some token Jewish paraphernalia.

In the atmosphere of fear that stalked the JAR, the actual circulation of the newspaper declined to virtual extinction in 1949–50. As was the way of things in the Soviet Union, there was no overt prohibition of Yiddish, but risk-averse people nevertheless preferred to keep a distance from it. Birobidzhaners knew that licit was not synonymous with safe. It is hard, if possible, to measure the level of fear among Jews in various areas of the Soviet Union. Presumably, however, in Birobidzhan it was particularly high insofar as no other place was so spectacularly affected by the arrests of Jewish functionaries and intellectuals. Numerous Yiddish books at the regional library had been destroyed, and the museum of local history had been stripped of the department of Jewish culture. Also closed was the Yiddish theater named after Lazar Kaganovich, as well as the amateur Yiddish troupes. Yiddish had disappeared from all educational institutions of the region.[30]

This remains a secret of Soviet decision-making: what could be the precise reasons that Stalin had for destroying not only the Mikhoels-chaired JAFC, but the Yiddish culture altogether, notwithstanding that its active constituency was prevailingly loyal to Soviet Communism and had been declining anyway? It is more or less graspable why JAFC had got under the hammer. Established with a remit to generate propaganda products, it—to dismay of watchful ideological overseers—developed features of a centralized, internationally-linked (and hence, through the prism of paranoid delusion, conspiratorial) quasi-civil society organization. A body of this kind was doomed to disappear from the landscape of Soviet organizations. Nonetheless, other reasons should motivate the destroying of virtually the entire infrastructure of Yiddish culture, which previously, especially before 1938, the year of closing vital cultural and educational programs in minority languages, was generously sponsored by the state. By the end of the 1940s, however, any activity in Yiddish began to be considered at least potentially nationalist. In the country, where people had been preventively and routinely sentenced because of "*suspicion* of espionage" or "*unproven* espionage" (Article 58-6 of the Criminal Code of the Russian Republic), difference between "potentially nationalist" and "nationalist" was of little or no importance.

Among the local intelligentsia imprisoned in the late 1940s and early 1950s was Buzi Miller. Shortly before being arrested, he was removed from his post of editor of *Birobidzhaner Shtern*.[31] It seems that local journalists were not considered reliable enough to act as

Figure 4.1 Buzi Miller. © Courtesy of Elena Sarashevskaia.

editor-in-chief and such a person was brought on secondment from Ukraine in 1949. It was Shaya Kozinski, who demobilized after the war with the rank of colonel and lived in Chernivtsi working there in the Ukrainian press. In 1940–41 he edited the Kyiv Yiddish daily *Der Shtern* (Star).

Accused of authoring and publishing "politically harmful," "bourgeois nationalist" works, Miller served almost seven years in the Gulag, before returning to the city in 1956. On September 14, 1956, the local court officially rehabilitated him as well as the actor Faivel Arones, and the writers Israel Emiot (Goldwasser), Gessel Rabinkov and Luba Vasserman. Earlier, in November and December 1955, several other literati were rehabilitated, including the poet Chaim Maltinsky, the critic Shmuel Klitenik (posthumously), and the journalists Mikhail Fradkin and Naum (Nokhim) Fridman. In various years, the latter two edited *Birobidzhaner Shtern*. Soon after Miller's liberation, the Writers Union reinstated his membership, and invited him to Moscow to attend a cultural event marking the 40th anniversary of Sholem Aleichem's death.[32] Miller would live in Birobidzhan until his death in 1988, being cherished as the major local writer, a symbol of Yiddish culture in the JAR. One of the streets in Birobidzhan carries his name.

CHAPTER 5
AN ALMOST-LOST WORLD
OF JEWISH LIFE

Very little information came from Birobidzhan in the 1950s, though the Soviet propaganda apparatus used some opportunities to spread misleading statements. Thus, in a booklet about a visit of an American labor delegation, published in Moscow in 1953, one can read that the guests learned about the JAR as "the place where Jewish culture and religion is most extensively developed."[1]

After closing down *Eynikayt* in November 1948, the JAR did not warrant a mention in the Soviet press, except in such materials as post-election lists of deputes of the Supreme Soviet. After 1946, the region usually had one Jew in its constitutionally guaranteed five-person decorative parliamentary representation.[2] Shifra Kochina, a horticultural brigade leader, and Rakhil Freidkina, an agronomist, both from Valdgeim, filled the quota in 1946–1950 and 1954–1958. Vera Gleizer, a World War II veteran and a pedagogue who headed an orphanage established in 1957, represented the region in 1958–1962. Birobidzhan did surface in some Soviet newspaper articles, being referred to as one of the towns in the far eastern part of Russia, without indication of its belonging to the JAR. Neither Freidkina nor any other JAR residents figured on the list of distinguished Soviet Jews whose orchestrated collective letter in *Pravda* on November 6, 1956, condemned the "aggression of Israel, England and France against Egypt" in 1956, during the Suez Canal crisis.

The JAR remained almost invisible in the media also because, from 1949 to 1955, there was no industrial development in the JAR and no significant investments were made in the agricultural sector considered inefficient. Characteristically, in 1952 (in other sources 1953) the government issued a decree about *assisting*—rather than developing—the agricultural sector of the JAR. Meanwhile, the population of the

JAR was declining as people were leaving for better paid jobs and less remote regions.

In May 1951, a (British) *Observer* article by Edward Crankshaw carried the news that the Kremlin had merged the JAR into the Khabarovsk Krai, thus downgrading it into a region "administered as an integral part of the Russian Federated Republic."[3] An intelligence officer at the British Military Mission in Moscow in 1941–43, Crankshaw later turned to journalism and built a reputation of an expert on the Soviet Union. Yet, on this occasion, he was mistaken in his conclusions. The official status of the JAR remained the same as in 1934. The rumor, however, prevailed over the facts. A 1954 article by Maurice Friedberg, a specialist on Soviet literature, also mentions the "abolition" of the JAR.[4] The *American Jewish Year Book*, published annually by the American Jewish Committee, reported in its 1954 volume that nothing had been heard for years about Jewish life in the JAR and that, according to rumors, the territory had been transformed into an area of slave labor camps. There was an element of truth in this: political and criminal prisoners had built a number of objects in the JAR and, in 1945–49, the region housed camps for Japanese POWs. Even so, regular citizens, rather than camp inmates, made up the core majority of the region's population.

In September 1954, Hershl Weinrauch, known also as Grigory Vinokur and Hersh Vaynroykh, who in 1932–38 worked as a journalist in Birobidzhan, appeared as a witness before the US House Committee on Communist Aggression. In the post-war 1940s, Weinrauch managed, somehow, to leave the Soviet Union together with the repatriates to Romania and then briefly lived in Israel before moving to the USA. The House Committee learned from him that "Birobidzhan was fake" and that Soviet authorities "didn't officially liquidate it, but they closed the Jewish schools and eliminated Jewish cultural life."[5]

The dream of building a model city also remained unfulfilled. Leonid Leshchinskii, born in Birobidzhan in 1945, recalled:

> In the end 1940s and early 1950s, it was a little town composed mainly of two-story wooden barracks. Three streets—named after Kalinin, Lenin and Sholem Aleichem—crossed the town

center. Only one brick house, with flats for top functionaries, had running water, central heating and sewage ...

The Bira River would flood the entire town. There were two plants, one of them produced horse-carts and later lorry trailers [in the 1960s it was transformed into the largest local enterprise, the agricultural machinery plant Dalselmash], while the other plant produced metal constructions.

People lived poorly, getting by in large measure on what they could glean from their private allotments and farm animals. Practically all kept cows, pigs and chickens.[6]

Similarly, Radik Sandik, later a top administrator in Birobidzhan, remembers that in 1948 it was "a town of two-story wooden barracks interspersed with few and far between brick buildings (such as a school, the movies theater and the edifice of the regional Party committee) and several cobbled streets in the town center."[7] A Leningrad geologist who in 1954 spent several months in the JAR and portrayed Birobidzhan as "a usual provincial little town" with "several factories and produce cooperatives," was impressed by the state of affairs in the collective farm, named 20 Years of October (meaning the October 1917 revolution), all or almost all of whose members were Jewish. Their industry and resourcefulness determined success in running the farm. Apart from the "usual vegetables," they cultivated watermelons, melons, grapes and even cork trees.[8] This collective farm, situated in the village of Ptichnik (Chicken Farm), close to the outskirts of Birobidzhan, merged with the collective farm in Valdgeim to become part of the best-known collective farm of the JAR, Legacy of Lenin.

This farm was chaired by Vladimir Peller, a heroic World War II veteran. Riva Vishchinikina, a member of the farm, filled the Birobidzhan "Jewish quota" in the Soviet parliament in 1962–1966. Peller, who had demobilized as a Full Cavalier of the Order of Glory and in 1966 became a Hero of Socialist Labor (the highest civilian award), would fill this quota in 1970–1974. In 1971–1976, he was one of the two Jewish members of the Communist Party's Central Auditing Commission, the group one step lower in prestige than the Central

Committee. Peller was one of the seven JAR residents named Heroes of Socialist Labor, but only one more of them was Jewish: Haya Karasik, a seamstress at a local textile factory, who had lived in Birobidzhan since 1932.

Soviet statistical indicators regarding the occupational structure of the Soviet Jewish population reveal a certain peculiarity: whereas during the period 1959–1989 the proportion of Jews living in villages had declined from 4.7 to 1.2 percent, the same years show a rise, from 700 to 1,000, in the number of Jews heading agricultural estates, most notably collective farms or state farms. A few of them were named Heroes of Socialist Labor. The glass ceilings of various heights which, mainly from the late 1940s, limited career advancement of Soviet Jews, were not necessarily a hindrance in the case of a person who proved to be an effective and reliable *khoziaistvennik*, or manager. In the JAR, the Jews generally had better opportunities to be promoted to senior positions.[9]

In the mid-1950s, description of the "fertile land" in the Birobidzhan area began to appear in the Soviet press.[10] Nikita Khrushchev, the leader of the Communist Party and Soviet government from 1955 to 1964, mentioned Birobidzhan, without specifying its "Jewishness," as an area rather than a town: "Let's take, for instance, Birobidzhan. Rice has been cultivated there, watermelons and melons can grow, tomatoes, orchards! This is a wonderful place! It means that we have to move there. When? We'll discuss it, we'll see."[11] The issue of Birobidzhan, however, remained of passing interest to Khrushchev and his administration. André Blumel, a well-known figure in the French Socialist and Jewish circles, who as vice-president of the France-USSR Friendship Society had numerous contacts with Soviet officials, came to the conclusion that top Soviet functionaries neither truly knew nor cared about the situation of the Jews, this being considered as a minor issue, at least in the 1950s.[12]

A conversation with Khrushchev in August 1956 had left Joseph Baruch (Joe) Salsberg, a Canadian political activist, with a bad taste. During a meeting in Moscow, Salsberg was appalled to hear the Soviet leader's derogatory off-the-cuff remarks about Jews. Khrushchev's stereotype included such "Jewish traits" as laziness, untrustworthiness and clericalism. Khrushchev also did not hide his disappointment about the very poor results of the Birobidzhan drive. (Earlier, Salsberg and other members of the Canadian Communist delegation learned from the Soviet top functionaries that only Birobidzhan-based Jews represented a community, whereas in all other parts of the country the authorities treated Jews "like all other Soviet citizens").[13] According to a CIA "source," who apparently was present during the meeting, Khrushchev said that:

> the Soviets had given the Jews Birobidjan, an immense country with untold riches, and yet the Soviets cannot get the Jews to go there. Further, the Jews insist on returning to places from which they originally came. He stated the Soviets have had to send Russians and other nationalities to Birobidjan because not enough Jews are going there to cultivate the country.[14]

Two years later, Khrushchev's interview, published in the Parisian *Le Figaro* under the headline "The Jews Do Not Know How to Organize Themselves Collectively," made the Soviet leader look, in the words of the American public thinker Irving Howe, like "a vulgar anti-Semite."[15] Khrushchev said the following:

> How many Jews remain in this beautiful region? In the absence of any documents before me, I would not be able to give you a precise figure. In actual fact, there must be quite a large number there. Look, in 1955, I myself passed through Birobidzhan. And ... I noticed many signs in Yiddish there, in the stations and in the streets around the stations. This being granted, if one looks at the balance sheet, it is only right to conclude that Jewish colonization in Birobidzhan has resulted in failure. They alight there burning with enthusiasm, then, one by one, they return.
>
> How can one explain this disagreeable phenomenon? In my opinion, by historical conditions. The Jews have always preferred the trades of craftsmen. ... But, if you take building or metallurgy—mass professions—you might not, to my knowledge, come across a single Jew there.[16] They do not like

collective work, group discipline. They have always preferred to be dispersed. They are individuals.[17]

It seems that Khrushchev saw the fiasco of the Birobidzhan project as proof that the Jews, at least the majority of them, had already assimilated or were prone to do so. A believer in the rapid advancement to Communism, he certainly regarded this as a positive development. Nahum Goldmann, president of the World Zionist Organization and the World Jewish Congress, suggested sarcastically to welcome Khrushchev's remarks as a recognition of the fact that "the Jews of the Soviet Union constitute a nationality, separate and distinct from other nationalities in the Soviet Union, and that this nationality does not live in similar conditions to the other nationalities of the USSR."[18]

Soviet ideologists realized that Khrushchev's uncareful words had caused an undesirable reaction in many quarters of Western society. The article "Jewish Autonomy," bylined V. Pakhman and published in the Moscow newspaper *Sovetskaia Rossiia* (Soviet Russia) on August 6, 1958, aimed squarely at calming the Western public's concerns. This piece was the first description of the JAR in the Soviet press since the late 1940s. On August 11, the British Embassy in Moscow reported that the article had broken "the virtual blackout on news of the life of the Jewish community at Birobidjan." The report went on to state:

This glowing account does not bear much comparison with the impressions received by visiting foreigners. [The first secretary of the British embassy Edward E.] Orchard, who was in Birobidjan in March 1957, was told that Jews were drifting from the oblast [region] to the town and from the town to more developed parts of the Soviet Union. No effort had been made to rebuild the synagogue which had been destroyed by fire. The Yiddish newspaper [*Birobidzhaner*] *Shtern* was sold only under the counter; the date of the last book published in Yiddish [in Moscow rather than in Birobidzhan] was 1948. No works of Sholom Aleichem were in stock in the town's main bookshop. A year and a half ago the Birobidjan experiment was still the dismal failure which it has been since its inception.[19]

Pakhman's article presented a different picture, contrasting the happy life of Birobidzhan Jewish residents with the unhappiness of those erstwhile Birobidzhan residents who, "under the influence of Zionist propaganda, left for Israel." According to Pakhman, Israeli authorities treated all immigrants as unwelcome guests, while being particularly hostile to those who had arrived from the Soviet Union, other countries of the Communist bloc and India. Pakhman asserted, as if he had witnessed it with his own eyes, that the immigrants were crammed in barracks, often could not find work, dragged out a half-starved existence and got scoffed at by local Jews all the time.

In clear contradiction to Khrushchev's claim that the Birobidzhan project had not fulfilled its purpose, the article portrayed the JAR in glowing terms. Jews appeared in it in several different capacities: Iosif Bumagin , the fallen brave Red Army soldier awarded the title of Hero of the Soviet Union, Iosif Bokor, the head of the Birobidzhan city Communist Party organization, and Naum Korchminsky, editor of *Birobidzhaner Shtern*. Pakhman claimed with a good deal of exaggeration that Miller's name was "known far beyond the borders of Birobidzhan."[20]

In February 1959, in a small-talk conversation with the British Prime Minister Harold Macmillan, Khrushchev more or less repeated, even if in a milder form, his 1958 statement about Jews which echoed Stalin's 1945 remark:

An experiment had been made in settling them in their own area but this was mainly agricultural. The Jews were chiefly tradesmen and artisans and the experiment had not been very successful and there were few Jews left there. Jews were very talented; some of them were engaged in atomic and rocket research.[21]

Meanwhile, Pakhman's article provoked a paradoxical reaction. Harry Schwartz, a journalist on the *New York Times*, mentioned "speculation in some Jewish circles" in America that "the decision to paint a glowing picture of Jewish life in Birobidzhan may be intended to initiate a new campaign to induce Soviet Jews to move to that area."[22] It did not take long before Jewish organizations received "reliable information" from Israeli sources that "the Soviet Jews appeared in peril of their lives," because the Soviet government was purportedly considering a massive forced resettlement of Jews to the JAR. Furthermore, the same source claimed that the plan would be placed before the 21st Congress of the Soviet Communist Party convened on January 27, 1959.[23] In the Israeli view of the time, concentration of Jews in Birobidzhan was one of the options considered by the Soviet decision makers.[24] Impenetrability of the Soviet political kitchen sparked guesswork and conspiracy theories.

In reality, the 21st Congress did not have a Jewish resettlement on its agenda, but had to adopt a plan of economic development, with an emphasis, in particular, on strengthening the economy in Siberia. The Siberian agenda might form the "factual basis" for the disturbing rumors about a planned expulsion.[25] The hearsay about forced removal of Jews to Birobidzhan echoed the deeply resonant, if historically unsubstantiated, narrative about the deportation of Jews, which, according to a stubborn myth, failed to occur only because Stalin died before he could make it happen.[26] (A fleeting rumor about expulsion to Birobidzhan of "recalcitrant" Jews had currency also in the early 1970s.)[27]

The 1958–59 rumor had been put in circulation outside the country and remained hardly known to Soviet Jews, unless someone heard this in a foreign broadcast. Even those foreign observers who gave the rumor credence often remained unconvinced that the Soviets had in mind an all-embracing deportation. They were more prepared to believe that the government could organize a campaign of partly cajoling and partly browbeating some Jews, particularly young, to make them agree to move "voluntarily" to the Far Eastern region. Yet even a milder version of the predicted plan caused serious consternation. In 1956, Israel's Prime Minister David Ben-Gurion posited that if the Soviets sent a million Jews to Birobidzhan it would be tantamount to destroying Israel.[28] In the meantime, the Soviet propaganda machine once again played vigorously the Birobidzhan card. On June 13, 1958, the New York Yiddish daily *Der Tog* (The Day) quoted Khrushchev who said that "all the Jews could go to Birobidzhan and set up a Jewish state, but he was not prepared to allow Yiddish schools to be established all over Russia."[29]

On January 14, 1959, the Soviet Ambassador to the United Kingdom received a memorandum of the Anglo-Jewish Association on "Reported Renewal of Settlement of Soviet Jews in Birobidjan." An influential organization of the British Jewish establishment, the association urged "that no transfers of populations by compulsion, direct or indirect, of Jews or others be undertaken in the Soviet Union."[30] A day later, representatives of the American Jewish Committee, established in 1906 by people concerned about pogroms in Russia, had a meeting with Anastas Mikoyan, the First Deputy Chairman of the Council of Ministers and, generally, one of the central figures surrounding Khrushchev. This unprecedented encounter became a momentous episode in Soviet Jewish history. Never before had representatives of a Jewish organization been given a chance to meet with a visiting top Soviet official to discuss the situation of Soviet Jews. Mikoyan came to test the water before Khrushchev's historical visit to the United States in September 1959. The American press dubbed Mikoyan the "only man in the Kremlin with whom Washington could speak."[31]

Mikoyan, an Armenian, was not directly involved in defining policy towards Jews. However, his name appeared for a while on the JAR map. In 1945, a new settlement, named Mikoyanovsk, emerged at a site of tin deposits. The toponym might have been a present for Mikoyan's 50th birthday. However even this tenuous link between him and the JAR had disappeared after the September 1957 decree, which banned naming towns, streets, etc. after live people. Since then, the settlement of Mikoyanovsk has been known as Khingansk, by the name of the Khingan River, a tributary of the Amur.

Like the Anglo-Jewish Association, the American Jewish Committee did not represent a mass-based constituency but was made up largely of prominent and wealthy individuals. Among the committee's four representatives who participated in the meeting with Mikoyan were Herbert H. Lehman, the former New York governor and senator, and Jacob Blaustein, a prominent American entrepreneur.[32] The memorandum, written on January 2, 1959 by Eugene Hevesi, who served as foreign affairs secretary for the American Jewish Committee, outlines the background knowledge that the four American Jewish establishment figures possessed about the plan, "discovered by Israeli intelligence in Russia" (most probably, by the Nativ, "path," a 1952 established agency for covert activities in the Soviet Union and other Communist countries) and relayed to the committee confidentially by some official Israeli sources:

> The only further detail that the Israelis could add to this information was some indication that the Soviet authorities may apply educational or economic "inducements" in furthering the resettlement plan but would abstain from the use of direct administrative compulsion. For this reason, the Israelis urged us to avoid, in our public comments on the problem, any references to the possibility of compulsory "mass deportations," implying that any exaggeration on our part would make it easy for Soviet propaganda to brand our statement untrue.
>
> Meanwhile, circumstantial evidence was growing in confirmation of the news received from Israeli authorities.... Cairo Radio greeted the renewal of the idea of a "Jewish state" inside the Soviet Union with great satisfaction, and expressed the hope that Mr. Ben-Gurion himself would soon find his way there.[33]

Mikoyan flatly refuted the existence of a plan to start expulsions to the JAR and authorized Lehman to state to the press in no uncertain terms that the entire story was altogether false.[34] It remains unclear to what degree the American Jewish Committee, and the American public in general, took Mikoyan's words as truth or whether they did not believe him and considered themselves saviors of Soviet Jews. In fact, perhaps there was no smoke without fire: some people in the Kremlin corridors of power might have broached the idea of a limited-scale and not necessarily Jewish resettlement to JAR, encouraged and sponsored by the government. They could suggest it in an attempt to find additional human resources for the region.

The London *Jewish Chronicle* pointed to Mikoyan's decision to speak with Jewish representatives, on the eve of his meeting with

President Dwight D. Eisenhower, as a sign that the image-conscious Soviet leaders were fully aware that they could not disregard the reaction abroad to their policy concerning the Jews. It also opined that, following his American visit, Mikoyan might "advise the Kremlin of the need for greater discretion in the handling of Jewish affairs."[35] Indeed, the experience brought from Mikoyan's encounters in America caused a change in the Soviet leadership's views on reviving Yiddish publishing. It is beyond a coincidence that a collection of Sholem Aleichem's stories, the first Yiddish book in the post-Stalinist period, came out in Moscow with remarkable speed of preparation and production to mark the writer's birth centennial in March 1959. The book heralded a revival of regular publications in Yiddish. Two and a half years later, in August 1961, a literary journal *Sovetish Heymland* (Soviet Homeland) began to appear in Moscow. Miller became a lifelong member of the editorial board of the journal. Its editor, Aron Vergelis, had the regalia of "first poet of Birobidzhan." In his autobiography, he wrote that his brother was the organizer of a state farm there and he himself worked as a cow herder under him.[36]

By the strictest criteria, Emmanuil Kazakevich rather than Vergelis was the first poet of Birobidzhan. Kazakevich also had a much more impressive record as a war veteran, using his experiences as the basis of his Russian novels. After the success of his 1947 debut novel *Star*, he reinvented himself as a successful Russian novelist and henceforth did not write in Yiddish, thus leaving the vacant poetic throne of Birobidzhan to Vergelis. After Kazakevich's death 1962, his name was given to one of the streets of Birobidzhan. This was the second time that a Kazakevich Street appeared in the town. In 1935, a street was named after Kazakevich's father, Henekh, editor of *Birobidzhaner Shtern*, who deceased in that year. In 1938, however, his name, closely associated with the circle of Liberberg's friends, was removed from the town's map.

In 1959, soon after Mikoyan's return from America, Max Frankel, then a Moscow-based journalist of the *New York Times*, brought back from Birobidzhan pleasant memories of eating gefilte fish with horseradish and cheese blintzes with sour cream. This did not help him to find any indication that the city anticipated the arrival of new settlers: "The Soviet government has denied rumors abroad that it intends to direct more Jews to the province. There is no evidence of such plans in Birobidzhan."[37] Probably, this was why the Soviet authorities allowed a foreign journalist to visit the city: to convey to the American public that he could not detect any Jewish in-migrants, let alone forced re-settlers. A correspondent of the New York *Forverts* spoke with a Birobidzhan dweller who had repatriated to Poland in 1959 and learned from him that he never heard of any new resettlements to the JAR or of any preparation for such a campaign. Moreover, he saw a different direction of migration, namely *from* Birobidzhan.[38]

Frankel made interesting observations on mundane details of life in the city, which struck him as a rather agreeable place, with people dressed as elsewhere in the Soviet Union or perhaps a bit more stylish, thanks to locally produced shoes and accessories. Indeed, Birobidzhan had been selected to become the center of consumer manufacturing in the Soviet Far East. Local factories and produce cooperatives supplied the area with fabrics, garments, footwear and knitted goods. The newly built or expanded clothing and furniture factories, and the plants producing power transformers and agricultural machinery, created new positions of employment, but predominantly non-Jews, often recent arrivals to the region, filled new job openings.[39] Housing construction was also up in the region.

Frankel left the city with the impression that its job market did not appeal to young Jews. They often preferred to leave for education and career possibilities elsewhere, notably to Khabarovsk—many, if not the majority, of its Jews had "defected" there from the JAR—and returned "only to look up old girl friends." Indeed, Birobidzhan, a town without a university or other higher schools, could not be an appealing place for young people with strong educational values. The situation was different in other autonomous regions. Thus, in the Khakas region in Siberia and the Karachay-Cherkess region in the Caucasus (both are republics in contemporary Russia) there were pedagogical universities and academic centers for studying history, literature and linguistics. As for the JAR, higher educational institutions based in the neighboring city of Khabarovsk and in the Siberian cities of Tomsk and Novosibirsk were the magnets for talented school graduates. As a result of the brain drain and the nature of the local job market, by the end of the 1960s, the percentage of Jewish Birobidzhan residents with higher education was almost eight times lower than the average among the Soviet Jews.[40]

Frankel noted also that "no youngsters ever show up at the shack that serves as a synagogue. Friday nights and Saturdays, ... Cantor Kaplan (there is no rabbi) leads prayers for thirty persons, more women than men." He was told that on Yom Kippur the number of worshippers was much larger—four hundred, and that a few packages of matzo arrived from Israel each Passover. The Polish journalist Dominik Horodyński, who gave his impression of visiting Birobidzhan in a December 1958 article that appeared in the Warsaw weekly *Swiat* and then in his 1959 book of travel impressions in Siberia, had learned that the congregation numbered only 24, none of them were young, but "more than 50" used to come to the High Holidays.[41] A Birobidzhan dweller, a lifelong enthusiast of Hebrew, wrote in 1958 that he took part in a Passover seder for the first time in about 35 years. He added though that the majority of the Birobidzhaners who got matzo from other cities or baked it themselves were predominantly "uncouth and ignorant" people, who during the entire year normally bred pigs and did not observe the Sabbath.[42]

In 1961, two diplomats from the British embassy visited Birobidzhan. They found that it was:

in fact little more than a village, consisting largely of huts and unsurfaced roads. It is pleasantly, though probably unhealthily situated as it is surrounded by marshy land which breeds a particularly aggressive type of mosquito. A large proportion of the town's population is obviously Jewish but there are few signs of national culture. In the bookshops only Russian books were displayed and further efforts to discover what was available in Yiddish revealed that there was nothing more than a few school textbooks. Only a few people seemed to have any idea of the whereabouts of the synagogue. This was perhaps not very surprising since it is housed in a wooden hut similar to others in the same rather muddy road. The rabbi was away and the caretaker said that the services were attended by only a few, usually old, people.[43]

Judging by an article in a Soviet anti-religious journal, in the mid-1960s the Birobidzhan Jewish religious community had forty-three members ranging from 63 to 84 years old. A survey involving 300 Jewish city dwellers, "mainly those who for some reason could be considered religious," found only eight believers, all but one aged over 60. The author of the article, a sociologist, pointed to the fact that the builders of the JAR in the 1920s and 1930s were, as a rule, young secular enthusiasts, therefore religion did not take roots in the city. The number of worshippers during the Passover holiday had fallen from 300 in the 1940s and 1950s to about forty.[44]

The 1959 census brought some statistical clarity to the composition of the local population: 14,269 local Jews made up 8.8 per cent of the JAR's population and 0.7 per cent of the Soviet Jews; 5,597 of them claimed Yiddish as their first language. The relatively high proportion of Yiddish speakers among Birobidzhan Jews reflected the essentially negative fact that young people tended to leave the region. Jewish residents of the JAR tended to live in the town of Birobidzhan, where a quarter of the approximately forty thousand residents identified themselves during the census as Jewish. Close to a third of the deputies of the Birobidzhan city soviet (council) elected—or, given the reality of Soviet "elections," authorities-selected—in 1961 had Jewish-sounding names, which was a proportion twice as high as in the soviet of the JAR.[45] In 1959, compared with 1939, the Jewish population of the JAR had shrunk by 19 percent. This decline continued in the coming years. In 1969, the census recorded that the entire population of the JAR was 172,449 and of these only 11,452 were Jewish—or less than 7 percent. As a result, the Jews had slid to the third position among the largest population groups in the region, after the Russians and Ukrainians.[46]

CHAPTER 6
A PROPAGANDA FAÇADE

While Birobidzhan continued to appear intermittently in the Soviet agitprop's products crafted for credulous foreign readers with residual affection for the Far Eastern Jewish "homeland," it did not play any practical role in the self-identification of Soviet Jews. Significantly, after the late 1940s the agitprop did not make any meaningful effort to bridge culturally the Soviet Jewry with Birobidzhan, considering such efforts either futile or, probably, counterproductive as potentially nationalist. By the rule of the time, subscription to local newspapers was available only in the areas of their publication, in particular because of the fear that—as the state security maintained—they could provide fodder for analysts of foreign intelligence agencies. Thus, both *Birobidzhaner Shtern* and its Russian counterpart *Birobidzhanskaia Zvezda* remained invisible outside the JAR. An exception would be made as late as 1970, when *Birobidzhaner Shtern* became available to subscribers all over the country and abroad, following a special decision to use it as a counterpropaganda move in the anti-Zionist campaign.

In 1954, the existence of *Birobidzhaner Shtern* was confirmed by Harrison E. Salisbury, the first regular correspondent of the *New York Times* in post-World War II Moscow, who received permission to make a stopover in Birobidzhan. In one of his articles titled "Russia Re-Viewed" (the series received the 1955 Pulitzer Prize for international reporting), Salisbury stated that the Yiddish newspaper came out three times a week and, as he was told, had a circulation of one thousand copies.[1] While Salisbury received outdated information, the reality was more modest: only 500 copies of the paper would be printed (but not necessarily sold) at the time, whereas *Birobidzhanskaia Zvezda* boasted a circulation of 20,000.[2]

The local apparatus of government, including the agency known from March 1954 as the Committee for State Security, or KGB in the

Russian abbreviation, meticulously stage-managed the rare visits of journalists and diplomats. By Salisbury's account, during his visit he "was unable to take a single step in the streets of Birobidzhan without the company of the agents.... Their role was obvious. They were to make it evident to the local residents that I was being followed and that it was more healthy not to talk to me."[3] Foreigners would get a chance to talk almost exclusively to carefully-vetted people. Salisbury's visit was also meticulously orchestrated:

> Never during question periods, which uniformly occurred when this correspondent was escorted through schools, factories or other institutions, were questions asked about Jews abroad, Israel, Zionism or other matters of Jewish interest. Officials said this reflected a lack of interest on the part of Jews in such matters.[4]

In June 1956, Yosef Avidar, Israeli ambassador to Moscow, and his wife, Yemima Tchernovitz, used the unprecedented opportunity to spend a couple of days in Birobidzhan. Tchernovitz, a renowned Hebrew children's writer, described in her diary their visit to the editorial office of the Yiddish newspaper, where they were shown "a pitiful copy [i.e., translation] of the local Russian paper, which itself was a copy of *Pravda*."[5] While leading writers of central Soviet periodicals could make their journalism more or less readable, provincial newspapers usually filled their pages with reprints and dull articles describing achievements of local factories and collective farms. *Birobidzhaner Shtern* was in a particularly disadvantaged position, having an exceptionally limited choice of local people able and willing to work as Yiddish journalists.

Upon his return to Moscow, Avidar shared his observations with the British ambassador, who reported to London:

> He said his impressions could be summarized by saying that of the three words in the title of Birobidjan, only the last [i.e., "region"] had any reality. There was of course no question of autonomy, and there was very little that was really Jewish about the area. There was no school in which instruction was carried

on in Yiddish and Yiddish was not even taught as a language in any of the schools. There was no Jewish theater. In the bookshop in the capital of the area General Avidar could find only four books in Yiddish; the works of well-known Yiddish writers such as Sholem Aleichem were not available. There was one little paper in Yiddish which appeared twice a week; it was merely a reproduction of *Pravda*. There was one synagogue; this had been burnt down two months ago but General Avidar thought it was going to be repaired. Practically none of the Jewish children spoke or understand Yiddish, though the older Jews in the area seemed to speak it among themselves.

...His impression was that there was a much higher proportion of Communists among the Jews of Birobidjan than in other Jewish communities which he has come across here in places like Kiev [Kyiv] and Homel [Gomel, the second largest city in Belorussia].[6]

It remains unknown if the several lovers of Hebrew, who visited the Israeli ambassador and his wife at the hotel, did it by their own initiative, or—which seems to be more probable—knowingly or inadvertently acted as extras in a performance set up by the KGB for the foreign guests.[7]

In the summer of 1956, after learning that the foreign press cited material published in Birobidzhan, local functionaries raised alarm and reported the perturbing problem up the chain of command to the Central Committee of the Communist Party, pointing to the Warsaw Yiddish paper *Folks-Shtime* (People's Voice) as the source of the information leak. In fact, the Warsaw editors, veterans of the Communist movement, meant well: their reprint of an article from *Birobidzhaner Shtern* and the reproduction of the post-mark bearing the official stamp of the JAR intended to refute the claims that the Birobidzhan area had lost its Jewish definition.[8]

To local officials' surprise and relief, Moscow functionaries issued an instruction that, instead of fencing itself hermetically off from the rest of the world, *Birobidzhaner Shtern* should expand contacts with "progressive Jewish newspapers." Soviet policymakers found it necessary to market around the world the events, publications and other activities, showing off achievements in the field of Yiddish culture. Foreign audiences used to get this kind of information also in the 1920s and 1930s. Yet, back then the state sponsored Yiddish culture, first, for the domestic market—as part of programs aimed at solving social and economic problems of the Jewish population—and second, and only second, for making an impression abroad. In the 1950s and onward, foreign audiences were, as a rule, the main targets for publicizing various Yiddish projects. Moreover, such projects would get the authorities' consent mainly or even solely for the purposes of cultural counterpropaganda, aimed at rebuffing accusations of "alleged" restrictions for Jewish culture.

The reality-detached official propaganda line was that Birobidzhan represented an example or even apotheosis of the successful implementation of the Soviet nationalities policy towards the Jews. In this context, the issue of quality of publications in *Birobidzhaner Shtern* came to the fore. The result was that, in 1956, the newspaper began to appear three times a week with double the number of pages: four instead of two. A new equipment mechanized its typesetting, previously done by hand.[9] These changes, however, did not lead to tangible improvement in the content of the newspaper. Obviously, the staff journalists simply could not jump above their heads.

On his Moscow visit in 1958, Chaim (Henri) Sloves, a French Communist Yiddish writer, went to the Lenin Library (now the Russian State Library), where the Periodicals Department provided access to readers to recent issues of several Yiddish newspapers—*Birobidzhaner Shtern* and foreign Communist papers. In contrast to the foreign newspapers that were worn from being read over and over, the issues of *Birobidzhaner Shtern* looked completely untouched.[10] The contents of the Birobidzhan newspaper had not improved enough to become appealing to any significant number of local readers. A 1959 article by Max Frankel provided some details of its non-subscription distribution: "Two newsstands had a few copies; a third, placed near a publicly posted copy of the paper, had not heard of it."[11]

The orthography of *Birobidzhaner Shtern* reflected the results of the radical Soviet language-planning reforms of the 1920s and 1930s, which meant, in particular, the application of phonetic-morphological spelling to all Hebrew and Aramaic elements and the elimination of the word-final forms for five letters used in Hebrew and traditional Yiddish writing systems. Absence of the final letters remained a hallmark of *Birobidzhaner Shtern* during the entire Soviet period, even following the restoration of these letters in Moscow Yiddish publications. The reason was purely technical: the Moscow printing shop could print these letters, whereas the typographic equipment in Birobidzhan lacked them.

Birobidzhaner Shtern continued to pop up in the propaganda material prepared for foreign audiences. The person responsible for this was Solomon Rabinovich, a veteran Soviet Yiddish journalist who, after serving six years in the Gulag, worked in the Sovinformburo (from 1961, Novosti Press Agency), the parent organization for his pre-arrest employer—the Jewish Anti-Fascist Committee. Some of his articles contained journalistic portraits of happy Birobidzhan Jewish dwellers, working at various factories and organizations and enjoying Yiddish cultural events.[12] The CIA, which monitored Rabinovich's activity, noted in a memorandum that, from February 1959 to January 1960, he submitted eighteen articles for the New York *Morgn-Frayhayt*.[13] Mordechai Gutman of Kfar-Saba, Israel, wrote in his letter to the *New York Times*, published on September 2, 1959, that Rabinovich's hailing of Soviet life was "hardly admissible testimony," because the Moscow journalist was "a man shattered by the Soviet Secret Police, tortured in its slave labor camps and fearful of further persecution." Gutman knew Rabinovich "extremely well" at the time when they were both incarcerated in a camp near the coal-mining town of Vorkuta, north of the Arctic Circle.

In his pamphlet *Jews in the Soviet Union*, published in a few languages by the Novosti Press Agency, Rabinovich, who visited Birobidzhan "when the first settlers arrived, their luggage consisting of old pillows and ragged blankets," wrote in the 1960s:

It seems to me that one of the main reasons is this: by the end of the thirties, especially in the war years, there was no longer any need for Jews with jobs to move. Why should a person living in Vinnitsa [Vinnytsia], Kiev [Kyiv] or Sverdlovsk [now Ekaterinburg] leave a place where he has lived for a long time, give up his permanent job and abandon his friends and acquaintances? There may have been other reasons. And of course, Soviet power is not to blame for the fact that tens of thousands and not hundreds of thousands went to Birobidjan.[14]

The ethnic structure of Birobidzhan and the dearth of meaningful forms of Jewish cultural life remained sore points for Soviet propaganda. Paul Novick, who modified his views as he learned about the Stalinist repressions and ultimately was expelled from the American Communist Party for "nationalism," complained in the early 1970s that the Novosti Press Agency articles describing Jewish life in the JAR sounded so shaky that he could not use them in *Morgn-Frayhayt*, rebranded from Communist to "progressive."[15] In September 1970, Lev Shapiro, a functionary of Jewish origin appointed that year to serve as the JAR's Party boss, took part in a meeting of the Party organization of the *Birobidzhaner Shtern* convened to welcome the Communist Party Central Committee's recent decree about reinforcing the Yiddish newspaper. Nonetheless, no decree could turn it into a quality periodical. Novick's friend, Sid Resnick, who joined the American Communist Party in his youth but left it in 1967, wrote in the late 1970s about *Birobidzhaner Shtern*:

This is a good newspaper if one wants to find out how much cement or how many machine parts or stockings are produced in the local factories or what the scores are of the local athletic teams, but one will find little in it about Jewish affair, Yiddish literature or education.[16]

There were some attempts to add ethnic color to the JAR. The restaurant of the Birobidzhan hotel Vostok could serve a "dinner described as 'Jewish cuisine,' which included something that might be called Siberian gefilte fish, chicken soup and smoked salmon."[17] The Yiddish writer Tevye Gen, who lived in Birobidzhan in the 1930s, was at pains to paint an attractive picture of the city as he saw it during his short stay there in 1963. However, the resulting image came out bleak and, despite the writer's efforts, only superficially Jewish—in the name of Sholem Aleichem Street, in distinctly Jewish names of local residents mentioned in the narrative, and in the writer's flashbacks to the early years of the Birobidzhan drive.[18]

In December 1965, an amateur Yiddish dramatic circle emerged in Birobidzhan. It is not clear if that had happened thanks to a grassroots initiative or to the authorities' decision to have such a cultural institution in the JAR. Moyshe Bengelsdorf, the troupe's director, worked at the Birobidzhan State Yiddish Theater until its liquidation in 1949. In 1967 the troupe received the status of a "people's theater" and thus got access to the state's financial and other countenance. Grigory Gurevich, a Leningrad theater director who specialized in training directors of people's theaters and spent some time in Birobidzhan, praised the older group of actors, who—in Gurevich's opinion—were "almost professional." As for the younger generation, he found them "helpless, like little-literate amateurs."[19]

In 1977, several young people were sent to be trained as a replacement for the old cadre working on *Birobidzhaner Shtern*. Instead of doing it in Moscow, which still had experienced Yiddish specialists, the Birobidzhan group was attached to the Higher Party School in Khabarovsk, whose faculty had only one Yiddish man-of-letter, Semen Iablonovskii, editor-in-chief of *Birobidzhaner Shtern* in the first half of the 1950s.[20] Predictably, none of the graduates, including Leonid Shkolnik who edited the newspaper in the 1980s, learned to write professionally in Yiddish.

Meanwhile, Soviet propagandists did their utmost to find a use for Birobidzhan. A Birobidzhan pedigree loomed large in the biography of Aron Vergelis, hand-picked by the authorities to play the leading role in Soviet Yiddish life. Two decades later after the launch of his edited Moscow Yiddish journal, this would be one of the criteria for training (at the Rabbinical School in Budapest) and appointing Adolf Shaevich, a Birobidzhan-reared engineer, as the new chief rabbi of the Moscow Choral Synagogue. The Moscow-born choreographer Yurii Sherling had nothing to do with Birobidzhan before he landed the job of directing the Jewish Chamber Music Theater, created in 1977 as a

Birobidzhan-affiliated troupe, though in reality it was based in Moscow. Sherling was confided that his troupe had emerged as a propaganda reply to the Jackson-Vanik Amendment, introduced by the United States in 1974 in an attempt to force the Soviet government to release Jewish emigrants in exchange for favorable trade and credit arrangements.[21] In 1982, a colorful Yiddish primer came out—ostensibly for Birobidzhan pupils—under the imprint of Khabarovsk, though its five thousand copies had been typeset and printed in Moscow.

Vergelis rather than Lev Shapiro or any other representative of the JAR acted as the main mouthpiece of the Kremlin's policy towards Jews. Although the Moscow editor never visited Birobidzhan after the late 1940s, he did not miss mentioning his adolescence there as a school of endurance and resilience. In one of his poems Vergelis described himself as a "young daredevil, / who spent his life at a campfire" and did not think twice to go "with a knife at a tiger."[22] He preferred to see Birobidzhan as a symbolic place. According to a protagonist of his novel *Time*, the country tells her Jews:

> Do you want Birobidzhan? Do you need Birobidzhan? Here, take it! Take it as much as you want. Birobidzhan is written in the Constitution... Use it like other peoples use [their territorial units]. But if you don't need it, if you want to live with much more elbow room, then live—you are welcome to do it. It is up to you to choose. Your Birobidzhan will remain in the Constitution anyway.

To all appearances, this was the paraphrase of a master script written by Kremlin ideologists. The words of Vergelis's literary character were echoed in the Lev Shapiro's statement: "The creation of a Jewish autonomous region has made it possible for the Jews to have a national home which they can come to at any time or leave, if they like, and go to any part of the Soviet Union."[23] In 1990, Leonid Shkolnik, freed from ideological constraints by Mikhail Gorbachev's *perestroika*, offered a candid and sobering portrayal of the "national homeland":

Birobidzhan has been transformed from a once small, remote little hamlet to a modern major town, with a large Russian-speaking population of many thousands. Only a few occasional little islets of Jewish culture, a few street signs in Yiddish and a shop-front with the latest issue of *Birobidzhaner Shtern* remind visitors that they are in the center of the Jewish Autonomous Region, which today . . . is having to decide the main question of its future existence: to be or not to be?[24]

It is hard, if even possible, to find a measurement for the Birobidzhaners' Jewishness on the general Soviet Jewish scale. As early as 1958, Horodyński's impression gained in Birobidzhan was that Jewish patterns of daily life did not appear to have differed significantly from those of non-Jews, remaining prominently divergent only in some traits, such as the attitude to hunting: Jews did not hunt. Yet even this difference tended to wither away, together with the increase of mixed marriages.[25] Nikolai Borodulin, who grew up in the JAR and went to become a Yiddish master teacher in New York, recalled that in the 1980s he was surprised when an acquaintance, into whom he bumped on a Birobidzhan street, congratulated him with a holiday, though it was still a long time before the next anniversary of the October 1917 revolution. It turned out that the acquaintance meant Rosh Hashanah, the Jewish New Year. Nikolai had never before heard about this holiday.[26]

For all that, Viktor Evtushenko, a KGB officer who headed the local branch of the security agency, remembered that Birobidzhan appeared to him as a town "with a pronounced veneer of a shtetl." To his delight, though, its younger Jews did not seem to have any interest in Zionism. Only one of them, a student, got fired up with the idea of emigrating to Israel, but Evtushenko and his people swiftly detected and thwarted the student's activity. The young man's mother, who headed the secret sector (the so-called "first department") at one of the enterprises, helped the KGB "to bring him to his senses." It is doubtful that, given her position, she was not a member of the Communist Party.

In fact, every fifth adult Soviet Jew was a card-carrying Communist by the end of the 1980s. By that time in Birobidzhan, more than a quarter of card-carrying Communists were Jewish, although Jews made up

Figure 5.1 A Lenin monument in Birobidzhan. © Courtesy of Valery Gurevich.

somewhat over a tenth of the city's population. Disproportionately high was also the number of Jews in the key administrative and managerial positions.[27] Albert Axelbank's journalistic visit to Birobidzhan in 1976 led him to the conclusion that local Jews were:

> a breed apart. They are uniformly not dissidents and—unlike numbers of Jews in cities such as Moscow, Leningrad and Odessa—they do not wish to emigrate to Israel or elsewhere. Jews were the pioneers here. As a result, some self-glorification is evident. You get the impression that the Jews of Birobidzhan are very patriotic and loyal Soviet citizens.[28]

For all that, beginning from 1990 (by then the government eliminated emigration restrictions), the loyal citizens—hunters and non-hunters alike—and their offspring began to leave the country. According to the demographer Mark Tolts, among the Jewry of Russia's provinces the JAR provided an especially large percentage of emigrants to Israel. Tolts also compared the rate of emigration to Israel with the Human Development Index (HDI) in the Russian cities in 1996. The HDI, which is a UN measure of quality and longevity of living, and education and skills, was in Birobidzhan as low as in Jordan (88th place among countries of the world), whereas in Moscow the index was similar to that of the Czech Republic (33rd among countries of the world) and for St Petersburg it was similar to Latvia (50th place).[29]

Although other reasons rather than the call of historic homeland might dominate the motivation for moving to Israel, the mass departure from the JAR, once conceived as the Soviet/Russian Jewish homeland, made the failure of the entire project particularly evident. Among the emigrants was Leonid Shkolnik, a deputy of the Supreme Soviet in the final years of the USSR, who in 1970 addressed Golda Meir, Israeli Prime Minister in 1969–74, with the following poetic lines: "Menia spasat' ne nado, gospozha / Nam s vami, ia skazhu, ne po doroge, / Vam ne pomogut nikakie bogi, / Kogda cherny i mysli i dusha" (There is no need to save me, Madam, / Believe me, we are going different ways, / God is of little help to you, / If your thoughts and soul are dark).[30]

The Jewish population of the region underwent a very pronounced decline, from 8,900 during the last Soviet census in 1989 to 2,300 in 2002 and around 1,700 in 2010. According to the 2002 census, only about 1 per cent of the total number of Russia's Jews lived in the JAR and the share of Jews in this region fell to about 1.2 per cent of the total population. The high rate of decrease clearly reflected the particularly difficult socioeconomic situation in Russia's Far East, where Jews constituted only a small part in the general outmigration. Between 1989 and 2022, the population of the JAR, one of the most problematic regions in post-Soviet Russia in terms of quality of life, had declined by a third from 231,000 to 153,700. During the same period, the population of the city of Birobidzhan dropped from 83,600 to 68,800. Most of the non-Jewish migrants went to other parts of the country, whereas the Jews and ethnically non-Jewish or partly Jewish family members had another possibility—emigration abroad, especially to Israel.[31] Birobidzhan had lost many qualified specialists, including scores of physicians, and medicine in the region had not fully recovered decades later.[32]

CHAPTER 7
AFTERLIFE

Paradoxically, it was in the turmoil of the final years of the Soviet Union when a real chance emerged to elevate the constitutional status of the Jewish Autonomous Region to that of the Jewish Republic. Nonetheless, the JAR remained the only autonomous region in Soviet and then independent Russia, whereas all other autonomous regions became republics by the end of 1990. The leading figures of the JAR, who were interested in elevating the region's and consequently their own status, faced stiff resistance of the population and the lower-level administration, especially in the rural areas. *Birobidzhanskaia Zvezda* published letters expressing worries about the future of the region. The letters reflected the widely spread conviction that it was a conspiracy aimed at secession of parts of the Far East from Russia after creating a springboard for Israel's expansion.

In that climate, the authorities were circumspect about conducting a referendum and finally, by the end of 1991, wound up the whole process halfway: the JAR did not turn into a republic, but nevertheless was allowed to cut its umbilical cord to the Khabarovsk Krai. Thus, the ethnic composition of the region—by that time 96 percent Russian and only 3 percent Jewish—made the plan of republic a non-starter.[1] In addition, the local Jews, predominantly the city of Birobidzhan dwellers, were already in an emigration mood and little concerned about the status of the place they sought to abandon.

Since that time the regional administration has continued making efforts to emphasize the "Jewishness" of the region and thus justify its name and, crucially, to secure its independence from the Khabarovsk Krai. Some non-Jewish locals, too, became perceptive to the idea that as a result of growing up and living in the JAR they had developed an idiosyncratic quasi-Jewish Birobidzhan identity, becoming *evreitsy*, or a kind of Jews.[2] Advocates of this theory avoid discussing how and in which forms (apart from recipes of food and a few words of Yiddish derivation) the highly emasculated Jewish tradition of the "real Jews" could pass on to their non-Jewish friends, colleagues and neighbors.

Like in Russia in general, the Chabad-Lubavitch network had found a way to dominate the religious life in Birobidzhan, claiming that the *real* local Jewish population did not decline lower than 4,000. Eli Riss, who served as the local rabbi in the 2010s, was born in Birobidzhan, but grew up in Israel. In 2020, the Kharkiv-born rabbi Ephraim Kolpak, a son-in-law of the Khabarovsk rabbi, replaced Riss, who had received a position in Moscow, moving up in the Chabad-Lubavitch hierarchy.

Yiddish remains present in Birobidzhan, though only symbolically. Street signs use both Russian and Yiddish. The Sholem Aleichem Amur State University, formerly Birobidzhan State Pedagogical Institute (opened in 1989), used to have Yiddish classes. Elena Sarashevskaia, one of the former students, became a conscientious and committed editor of the Yiddish pages in the predominantly Russian-language *Birobidzhaner Shtern*. Amateur groups perform in Yiddish.

The architecture of the city of Birobidzhan did not create any specifically Jewish visual context.[3] To remedy this drawback, there were erected monuments including "a three-story-high menorah, a statue of Yiddish writer Sholem Aleichem [the city received it as a gift from China in 2004], and a fountain crested by a 'Fiddler on the Roof' figure: a simulacrum of a simulacrum, evidently copied from the cover of the 1964 cast album of the Broadway musical based on Aleichem's writings."[4]

Shelley Salamensky, a historian and writer, suggested to use the terms "Jewface" minstrelsy and "Jewfaçade" display for describing the practice of various, often exoticized types of performance, primarily by non-Jews, intended to convey notions of historical Jewish life and culture.

In contemporary Birobidzhan, Yiddish music concerts, theater, and Jewish-related performances and exhibits of various sorts take place frequently. A local television series focusing on Jewish culture has been produced, and in the early 2000s a Chabad rabbi posted to Birobidzhan conducted a weekly radio show on the Jewish religion. Several small museums, libraries, and archives in the area display Jewish cultural holdings, and the newspaper, which retains its Yiddish title, continues to print one page of news in Yiddish per week. Every other year, Birobidzhan hosts a Jewish cultural festival in which the regular schedule of activities is intensified and supplemented with performances by guests from Moscow.[5]

The Russian Prime Minister Dmitry Medvedev, who put his signature under the 2013 program offering financial inducements to bring foreign re-settlers to the JAR, apparently did not see it as part of a minstrelsy. Nevertheless, the program ended up little more than a performance: only several people came to Birobidzhan from Israel, including the parents of rabbi Riss.

All in all, the JAR serves as a place where Jews *used to live* and as such it deserves to carry its name. The map is full of toponymic fossils. For over six decades the JAR was a setting for carrying out and instrumentalizing a unique nation-building experiment, which is valuable as an instructive historical lesson and—as this book attempts to convey—cannot be fully understood out of context of the political and economic evolution in the Soviet Union and beyond. In a sense, the Birobidzhan experiment is going on in post-Soviet Russia. However, it has little to do with Jewish life and history any more.

NOTES

Introduction

1. Chaim Gildin, *Gezamlte verk*, vol. 1 (Kharkiv: Literatur un kunst, 1932), 11.

2. Jacques Silber, "Some Demographic Characteristics of the Jewish Population in Russia at the End of the Nineteenth Century," *Jewish Social Studies* 42.3/4 (1980): 269–280; Mark Tolts, "Ethnicity, Religion and Demographic Change in Russia: Russians, Tatars and Jews," in *Evolution or Revolution in European Population*, vol. 2 (Milan: EAPS and IUSSP, 1996), 165–179.

3. See Gennady Estraikh, *In Harness: Yiddish Writers' Romance with Communism* (Syracuse, NY: Syracuse University Press, 2005), 24.

4. Elise Kimerling, "Civil Rights and Social Policy in Soviet Russia, 1918–1936," *Russian Review* 41.1 (1982): 44.

5. Terry Martin, *The Affirmative Action Empire: Nations and Nationalism in the Soviet Union, 1923–1939* (Ithaca: Cornell University Press, 2001), 13–14.

6. See, e.g., Irina Voloshinova, "Istoriia evreiskogo pereseleniia v SSSR v 1920-e—1930-e gg," *Nauchnye trudy po iudaike* 3 (2012): 361–375; Valentina Moiseenko, "Krest'ianskie pereseleniia v 1920-e gody," *Demograficheskoe obozrenie* 2 (2016): 87–141.

7. Among them: Allan L. Kagedan, *Soviet Zion: The Quest for a Russian Homeland* (New York, 1994); Robert Weinberg, *Stalin's Forgotten Zion: Birobidzhan and the Making of a Soviet Jewish Homeland: An Illustrated History, 1928–1996* (Berkeley, 1998); Ber Boris Kotlerman, *In Search of Milk and Honey: The Theater of Soviet Jewish Statehood (1934–49)* (Bloomington, IN, 2009); Masha Gessen, *Where the Jews Aren't: The Sad and Absurd Story of Birobidzhan, Russia's Jewish Autonomous Region* (New York, 2016).

Chapter 1

1. Emanuel A. Goldenweiser, "Economic Conditions of the Jews in Russia," *Publications of the American Statistical Association*, 9.70 (1905): 238.

Notes

2. Moyshe [Moissaye J.] Olgin, *Mayn shtetl in Ukraine* (New York: M. Gurevich's Publishing House, 1921), 68.

3. The full title of the journal was *Tribuna evreiskoi sovetskoi obshchestvennosti* (Tribune of the Soviet Jewish community).

4. Erik van Ree, *The Political Thought of Joseph Stalin: A Study in Twentieth Century Revolutionary Patriotism* (London and New York: RoutledgeCurzon, 2003), 65.

5. See Estraikh, *In Harness*, 85.

6. Baruch Glasman, *Step un yishev: Bilder fun a rayze iber di yidishe kolonyes fun sovet-Rusland un Ukraine* (Warsaw: Kultur-lige, 1928), 226–229.

7. Allan L. Kagedan, "American Jews and the Soviet Experiment: The Agro-Joint Project, 1924-1937," *Jewish Social Studies*, 42.2 (1981): 153–164.

8. Boris D. Bogen, *Jewish Philanthropy: An Exposition of Principles and Methods of Jewish Social Service in the United States* (New York: Macmillan Co., 1917), 264.

9. David Shub, *Fun di amolike yorn: bletlekh zikhroynes* (New York: CYCO, 1970), 612.

10. See Gennady Estraikh, *Transatlantic Russian Jewishness: Ideological Voyages of the Yiddish Daily Forverts in the First Half of the Twentieth Century* (Brookline, MA: Academic Studies Press, 2020), 181.

11. Ibid., 201, 210–211.

12. Joseph Leftwich, *What Will Happen to the Jews?* (London: P. S. King, 1936), 161; Joseph Leftwich, *Israel Zangwill* (London: J. Clarke, 1956), 217.

13. Estraikh, *Transatlantic Russian Jewishness*, 165.

14. Joseph Roth, *The Wandering Jews* (London: Granta, 2001), 107.

15. Evelyn Morrissey, *Jewish Workers and Farmers in the Crimea and Ukraine* (New York: privately published, 1937), 40. For a panegyric on Kalinin, see, e.g., S. Dingal, "Tsen yor prezident," *Der Tog*, April 25, 1929, 3.

16. Robert Weinberg, "Biology and the Jewish Question after the Revolution: One Soviet Approach to the Productivization of Jewish Labor," *Jewish History* 21.3–4 (2007): 413–428.

17. Vasil S. Kuibida *et al.*, *Administratyvno-terytorial'nyi ustriï Ukraïny* (Kyiv: Secretariat of Ukrainian Government, 2009), 53.

18. Sergei A. Elizarov, *Formirovanie i funktsionirovanie sistemy administrativno-territorial'nogo deleniia BSSR* (Gomel: GGTU, 2009), 135.

19. Leyb Zinger, *Evreiskoe naselenie v Sovetskom Soiuze* (Moscow-Leningrad: Gosudarstvennoe sotsial'no-ekonomicheskoe izdatel'stvo, 1932), 116.

20. See Gennady Estraikh, "Itsik Fefer: A Yiddish Wunderkind of the Bolshevik Revolution," *Shofar* 20.3 (2002): 21.

21. Anna Shternshis, "Soviet and Kosher in the Ukrainian Shtetl," in Gennady Estraikh and Mikhail Krutikov, eds., *The Shtetl: Image and Reality* (Oxford: Legenda, 2000), 148.

22. "Says Five-year Plan Will Completely Change Jewish Life in Soviet Russia," *Jewish Daily Bulletin*, February 17, 1930, 4.

23. "900,000 Jews Need to be Colonized, Leader in Work Declares," *Jewish Daily Bulletin*, June 24, 1929, 5.

24. See, e.g., Allan L. Kagedan, "Soviet Jewish Territorial Units and Ukrainian-Jewish Relations," *Harvard Ukrainian Studies* 9.1–2 (1985): 118–32; Dian A. Amanzholova, "Iz istorii zemleustroistva evreev v SSSR," *Cahiers du monde russe* 45.1–2 (2004): 217–220.

25. See, e.g., Jonathan Dekel-Chen, "An Unlikely Triangle: Philanthropists, Commissars, and American Statesmanship Meet in Soviet Crimea, 1922–37," *Diplomatic History* 27.3 (2003): 353–376.

26. Evelina M. Vladykina, "Samuil Ber i evreiskaia obshchina dorevoliutsionnogo Khabarovska," *Istoriia i kul'tura Priamur'ia* 1 (2014): 18–20.

27. See, e.g., "Planning a Colony of 1,000,000 Jews," *The New York Times*, January 29, 1928, 56; "Siberia Colonization Plan May Help," *Jewish Advocate*, February 9, 1928, 6.

28. Abram Merezhin, "Perspektivy evreiskogo zemleustroistva v SSSR," *Tribuna* 1–2 (1928): 13.

29. "Views Colonization in Bureya, Siberia, As Necessity for Russian Jews," *Jewish Daily Bulletin*, February 28, 1928, 3.

30. Zalman Wendroff, "Vos di farblibene kolonistn dertseyln vegn Biro-Bidzhan," *Forverts*, January 10, 1929, 5.

31. Angela Rohr, "Puteshestvie po Bira-Bishanu," *Ogonek*, September 30, 1928, 10–11.

32. Cf. Paul R. Mendes-Flohr, "The Throes of Assimilation: Self-Hatred and the Jewish Revolutionary," *European Judaism* 12.1 (1978): 34–39.

33. Abram Merezhin, *O zaselenii Biro-bidzhanskogo raiona trudiashchimisia evreiami* (Moscow: Emes, 1928), 8–18.

34. Viktoriia V. Romanova and D. V. Korolev, "Iz istorii bor'by s antisemitizmom v EAO v 1935 g.," *Vlast' i upravlenie na Vostoke Rossii* 1 (2008): 1–8.

35. Menachem Kadyshevich, *Birobidzhan—strana bol'shikh vozmozhnostei* (Moscow: OZET, 1931), 9–10.

36. Alexander A. Troyanovsky, "Why Anti-Semitism?" *The Sentinel*, March 26, 1936, 8.

37. See, e.g., Sergo Bengelsdorf, *Zhizn' v evreiskoi kul'ture* (Kishinev: Elan Poligraf, 2007), 37–38.

38. Cf. Robert L. MacDonald, "A land without a people for a people without a land": Civilizing mission and American support for Zionism, 1880s–1929. PhD dissertation (Bowling Green State University, 2012), 13.

39. "Communists Revive Slogan of 'Jewish Land' in Bira-Bidjan," *Jewish Daily Bulletin*, January 14, 1929, 1; Abram Merezhin, "Problemy Birobidzhana i lozung 'V evreiskuiu stranu!'" *Tribuna*, February 1, 1929, 12–14.

40. Chaim Sloves, *In un arum* (New York: YKUF, 1970), 124–126.

41. Nathan Chanin, "Genose Khanin dertseylt vos yidn in Rusland redn vegn Biro-Bidzhan," *Forverts*, January 8, 1929, 2, 4.

42. Yurii Larin, *Evrei i antisemitizm v SSSR* (Moscow: Gospolitizdat, 1929), 184.

43. "Bira-Bidjan, where a Jewish State May Rise: National Geographic Society Describes Region," *The Detroit Jewish News*, October 4, 1929, 23; "National Geographic Society Describes Bira-Bidjan," *The American Jewish World*, October 4, 1929, 87.

44. B. Livitin, "Dr. Rozen dertseylt vegn di naye plener fun fargresern yidishe kolonizatsye in sovet-Rusland," *Forverts*, December 29, 1928, 5. "Dr. Rosen Skeptical about Siberian Plan," *The New York Times*, February 12, 1928, 62.

45. "Memorandum from Joseph C. Hyman to Messrs. Felix M. Warburg et al., January 28, 1929," JDC Archive, document NY AR2132 01142.

46. Zosa Szajkowski, "Budgeting American Jewish Overseas Relief (1919–1939)," *American Jewish Historical Quarterly* 59.1 (1969): 83–113.

47. *Educating for Life: New Chapters in the History of ORT*, ed. by Rachel Bracha, Adi Drori-Avraham, and Geoffrey Yantian (London: World ORT, 2010), 119–120.

48. Henry F. Srebrnik, *Dreams of Nationhood: American Jewish Communists and the Soviet Birobidzhan Project, 1924–1951* (Boston: Academic Studies Press, 2010), 14.

49. "Transport of Tractors and Tools Sent from America to Bira Bidjan Colonists," *The Sentinel*, March 29, 1929, 2.

50. *Birebidzhanish: kleyne antologye vegn der yidisher avtonomer gegnt*, ed. by D. Zalbefert (Vilna: Kletkin, 1925), 110; Sandra McGee Deutsch, *Crossing Borders, Claiming a Nation: A History of Argentine Jewish Women, 1880-1955* (Durham and London: Duke University Press, 2010),

165; Victor A. Mireļman, *Jewish Buenos Aires, 1890-1939: In Search of an Identity* (Baltimore: Wayne State University Press, 2018), 144–146.

51. Ruta M. Shats-Mar'iash, *Byľ, iav' i mechta: kniga ob ottse* (Riga: BOTA, 1995), 151.

52. "Grindungs-farzamlung fun gezelshaft Agroid far emigratsye keyn Biro-Bidzhan," *Haynt*, June 10, 1934, 2; "Poland Bars Biro-Bidjan News," *The Sentinel*, January 17, 1935, 13; Harry Schneiderman and Melvin M. Fagen, "Review of the Year 5695," *The American Jewish Year Book* 37 (1935–1936): 208.

53. Valentina Moiseenko, "Mezhdunarodnaia migratsiia v Rossii (SSSR) v kontse XIX—pervoi treti XX veka," *Demograficheskoe obozrenie* 4 (2017): 118.

54. Baruch Gurevitz, "The Liquidation of the Last Independent Party in the Soviet Union," *Canadian Slavonic Papers* 18.2 (1976): 178–186.

55. David Goldberg, "Prospects of a Far Eastern Jewish Republic Under Soviet," *The Boston Globe*, October 6, 1929, 55.

56. Marina Apterman, "To the Holy Land and Back: The Opposition of Two Zions in Russian-Jewish Literature of the 1930s," *Judaica Russica* 1 (2021): 8–9.

57. Tamara M. Smirnova, "LenOZET kontsa 1920-kh gg. v zerkale statistiki," in *Evrei Rossii, Evropy i Blizhnego Vostoka*, ed. by Varvara G. Bovina and Maksim O. Mel'tsin (St Petersburg: Institute of Jewish Studies, 2019), 295–301.

58. Y. S-m, "Der tirazh fun der gezerd-loterey," *Der Emes*, May 13, 1928, 2.

59. Chaim Weizmann, *Trial and Error* (New York: Schocken, 1966), 13.

60. Glazman, *Step un yishev*, 226–229.

61. Zivion, "Yidishe interesn," *Forverts*, August 24, 1929, 3.

Chapter 2

1. C. Ezerskii, "30 dnei v Biro-Bidzhane," *Tribuna* 12 (1928): 9–12; A. Kantorovich, *Za sotsialisticheskii Birobidzhan* (Moscow: Dal'giz 1933), 20.

2. Matvei B. Druianov, *Evreiskaia avtonomnaia oblast' (Birobidzhan)* (Moscow: Emes, 1934), 16. See also A. Kirzhnits, *Birofeľd* (Kazan: OZET, 1934).

3. Kantorovich, *Za sotsialisticheskii Birobidzhan*, 3.

4. Max Kiper, "Peredmova," in M. [Moyshe] Alberton, *Biro-Bidzhan: podorozhni vrazhennia* (Kharkiv: Knihospilka, 1930, 5.

5. "Minutes of Meeting of Executive Committee of the Joint Distribution Committee held at the office of Mr. Felix M. Warburg, 52 William Street, New York City, Thursday, December 4th, 1930, at 3:00 P.M," JDC Archive, document NY AR2132 03012; Irina Voloshinova, "Dinamika evreiskogo naseleniia v SSSR v 1920-1930 gg.," in *Materialy XX mezhdunarodnoi ezhegodnoi konferentsii po iudaike*, vol. 2 (Moscow: Sefer, 2014), 287.

6. Evgenii V. Guzman and Liudmila I. Gorbunova, "Opyt realizatsii gosudarstvennoi pereselencheskoi politiki na iuge Dal'nego Vostoka SSSR (na primere Evreiskoi avtonomnoi oblasti) v 20-30-e gg. XX v.," *Vlast' i upravlenie na vostoke Rossii* 4 (2012), 65–71.

7. B. Z. Goldberg, "Russia's Daniel Boones," *The American Jewish World*, November 23, 1934, 5.

8. "Rough Notes of Discussion with Dr. E. A. Grower re Agro-Joint Colonies in Russia—Jan. 20, 1932," JDC Archive, document NY AR2132 01287.

9. See Wolfgang von Weisl, "Jewish Colony Soviet's Wedge into Manchuria," *Jewish Daily Bulletin*, October 15, 1933, 6.

10. Nikolai S. Vas'kiv, "Otobrazhenie osvoeniia Birobidzhana v ukrainskom putevom ocherke 1930-kh godov," in *Istoriia evreiskoi diaspory v Vostochnoi Evrope*, ed. by M. O. Meltsin i A. N. Pilipenko (St Petersburg: Institute of Judaica, 2012), 98–99.

11. Elena Sarashevskaia, "Zhizn' kak den' i noch," *Birobidzhanskaia Zvezda*, December 26, 2014. https://www.gazetaeao.ru/zhizn-kak-den-i-noch/

12. Viktor Fink, *Evrei v taige* (Moscow: Federatsiia, 1930), 246; Kantorovich, *Za sotsialisticheskii Birobidzhan*, 21.

13. "Memorandum on Birobidjan from Moses A. Leavitt to the Members of the Administration Committee. June 2, 1944," JDC Archive, document NY AR2132 00658.

14. Rohr, "Puteshestvie po Bira-Bishanu," 11. Less than three years later Baskin died not reaching the age of 40. V. S. Gurevich and E. G. Marundik, "Lev Grigor'evich Baskin—upolnomochennyi Komzeta, osnovatel' Amurzeta," *Regional'nye problemy* 22.2 (2019): 70–76.

15. Mendel Osherowitch, *Vi mentshn lebn in Sovet Rusland: ayndrukn fun a rayze* (New York: n.p., 1933), 142–145.

16. A. Leybman, "Kommuna 'IKOR,'" in *Liudi birobidzhanskogo pokoleniia*, ed. by Elena Sarashevskaia (Birobidzhan: Publishing house "Birobidzhan," 2019), vol. 2, 10–66.

17. William J. Broad, "A Spy's Path: Iowa to A-Bomb to Kremlin Honor," *The New York Times*, November 12, 2007, A1, A10; Yurii A. Lebedev, "Novye dokumenty po istorii atomnogo proekta iz semeinogo arkhiva Geroia Rossii Zh. A. Kovalia," *Voprosy istorii, estestvoznaniia i tekhniki* 37.4 (2016): 702–735.

18. Mary M. Leder, *My Life in Stalinist Russia: An American Woman Looks Back* (Bloomington and Indianapolis: Indiana University Press, 2001), 23.

19. Ben Zion Goldberg, *The Jewish Problem in the Soviet Union: Analysis and Solution* (New York: Crown Publishers, 1961), 174.

20. Ibid., 185.

21. Peysekh [Paul] Novick, *Idn in Biro-Bidzshan: a bazukh in der Idisher oytonomer gegnt* (New York: ICOR, 1937), 83.

22. Ben Zion Goldberg, *The Jewish Problem in the Soviet Union*, 184.

23. David Khait, "Vstrecha na granitse," *Ogonek*, September 30, 1936, 22.

24. Robert Pinkhasov, Svetlana Danilova and Semen Krikheli, *Evrei bukharskie, gorskie, gruzinskie v vodovorote istorii* (Brooklyn: n.p., 2017), 277; Valerii Dymshits et al., *Gorskie evrei* (Moscow and Jerusalem: DAAT/Znanie, 1999), 125–126; Krista A. Goff, *Nested Nationalism: Making and Unmaking Nations in the Soviet Caucasus* (Ithaca: Cornell University Press, 2021), 30–31.

25. Evgenii Petrov, "Puteshestvie na Dal'nii Vostok," *Ogonek*, April 30, 1938, 19–20.

26. Druianov, *Evreiskaia avtonomnaia oblast'*, 5.

27. B. I. Trotskii, *Stroitel'stvo Evreiskoi avtonomnoi oblasti v 1935 i 1936 godakh* (Moscow: Emes, 1936), 7–10.

28. Iosef S. Brener and Aleksandr V. Zaremba, *Birobidzhanskii proekt v nauchnykh issledovaniiakh* (Kyiv: Zolotye vorota, 2013), 133.

29. See Gennady Estraikh, "David Bergelson in and on America," in *David Bergelson: From Modernism to Socialist Realism*, ed. by Joseph Sherman and Gennady Estraikh (Oxford: Legenda, 2007), 315.

30. Boris Kotlerman, "'Why I am in favour of Birobidzhan': Bergelson's Fateful Decision," in *David Bergelson: From Modernism to Socialist Realism*, ed. by Joseph Sherman and Gennady Estraikh (Oxford: Legenda, 2007), 140.

31. See Ber Boris Kotlerman, "The Image of Birobidzhan in Soviet Yiddish Belles Letters," *Jews in Eastern Europe* (2002): 51.

32. David Bergelson, *Birebidzhaner* (Moscow: Emes, 1934), 5–6.

33. Mykhailo Zhurba and Serhii Padalka, "Migration of the Jews from the Ukrainian SSR to the Jewish Autonomous Region (Birobidzhan) during the Second Half of the 1920s—First Half of the 1930s," *Skhidnoievropeiskyi istorychnyi visnyk* 17 (2020): 172.

34. Merezhin, *O zaselenii Biro-bidzhanskogo raiona trudiashchimisia evreiami*, 51.

35. *Dal'nii Vostok Rossii v epokhu sovetskoi modernizatsii: 1922—nachalo 1941 goda*, ed. by V. L. Larina et al. (Vladivostok: Dal'nauka, 2018), 81.

36. Fink, *Evrei v taige*, 270.

37. Bergelson, *Birebidzhaner*, 147–148.

38. Ber Boris Kotlerman, *In Search of Milk and Honey: The Theater of "Soviet Jewish Statehood" (1934–49)* (Bloomington: Slavica Publishers, 2009), 143.

39. *Vospominaniia o E. Kazakeviche*, ed. Galina O. Kazakevich i B. C. Ruben (Moscow: Sovetskii pisatel', 1979), 31–33, 45–52.

40. G. D. [Hirsh] Bloshtein, *Birobidzhanskie zarisovki* (Moscow: Emes, 1934), 11.

41. Hirsh Bloshtein, "Tsum ratnfarband," *Frayhayt*, November 12, 1926, 4.

42. David Bergelson and Emmanuil Kazakevich, *Birobidzhan: an algemeyne iberzikht fun der yidisher avtonomer gegnt* (Moscow: Emes, 1939), 13–14.

43. Lord Marley, *Biro Bidjan as I Saw It* (New York: ICOR, 1935), 5.

44. Iosef S. Brener, "Gorod, kotoryi ne byl postroen: shveitsarskii arkhitektor Khannes Maier i ero proekt 'evreiskogo sotsgoroda' u podnozhiia Malogo Khingana," in *Mizreh: Jewish Studies in the Far East* (Frankfurt am Main: Peter Lang, 2009), 133–134.

45. Fink, *Evrei v taige*, 232.

46. Ben Zion Goldberg, *The Jewish Problem in the Soviet Union*, 181–182.

47. Shifra Lifshitz, *Khaloymes un virklekhkayt: Biro-Bidzhan un arbets-lagern* (Tel Aviv: Eygns, 1979), 65, 70.

48. Svetlana V. Kutovaia, "Formirovanie sotsial'nogo prostranstva Evreiskoi avtonomnoi oblasti v 1928–1990 gg," *Regional'nye problemy* 14.1 (2011): 113.

49. Leder, *My Life in Stalinist Russia*, 17.

50. David Bergelson, *The Jewish Autonomous Region* (Moscow: Foreign Languages Publishing House, 1939), 27.

51. Osher Perelman, *Birobidzhan: shilderungen fun a rayze in yuli-oygust 1934* (Varshe: Groshn-bibliotek, 1934), 59.

52. Novick, *Idn in Biro-Bidzshan*, 18.

53. Petrov, "Puteshestvie na Dal'nii Vostok," 18.

54. Evgenii I. Vaneev, *Biro-Bidzhan: istoricheskaia spravka, geografiia, prirodnye bogatstva, puti soobshcheniia, naselenie, khoziastvo, kolonizatsiia* (Khabarovsk: OGIZ, 1931), 82; Kadyshevich, *Birobidzhan—strana bol'shikh vozmozhnostei*, 9–10, 30; Kantorovich, *Za sotsialisticheskii Birobidzhan*, 48.

55. Liudmila S. Lisitsyna, "Prichiny razvitiia legkoi promyshlennosti v seredine 1940-kh—seredine 1950-kh gg. v iuzhnykh raionakh Dal'nevostochnogo regiona," *Izvestiia Altaiskogo gosudarstvennogo universiteta* 4.1 (2010): 160–164.

56. Emmanuil Kazakevich, *Groyse velt: lider, poemes un geshikhtes* (Moscow: Emes, 1939), 133.

57. Alexander Ivanov, "Facing East: The World ORT Union and the Jewish Refugee Problem in Europe, 1933–38," *East European Jewish Affairs* 39.3 (2009): 376.

58. Igor Krupnik, "Soviet Cultural and Ethnic Policies towards Jews: A Legacy Reassessed," in *Jews and Jewish Life in Russia and the Soviet Union*, ed. by Yaakov Ro'i (Ilford, Essex, and Portland, OR: Frank Cass, 1995), 75–76.

59. Joseph Stalin, *Marxism and the National and Colonial Question* (Moscow: Foreign Languages Press, 1934), 8.

60. Mikhail I. Kalinin, *Ob obrazovanii Evreiskoi avtonomnoi oblasti* (Moscow: Emes, 1935), 6–7, 10–11, 13–14.

61. Abulkasim Lakhuti, "Oktiabr´skoe voskresenie narrodov," *Literaturnaia gazeta*, June 30, 1935, 4.

62. "Doklad tov. Stalina I. V. o proekte konstitutsii Soiza SSSR," *Izvestiia*, November 26, 1936, 3.

63. Jacob Lestschinsky, "Der skandal mitn Biro-Bidzhan blof, velkher hot farumglikt fil yidishe familyes in Poyln," *Forverts*, February 8, 1935, 6, 8; idem, "Ken Biro-Bidzhan farbesern di lage fun di yidn in sovet-Rusland?" *Forverts*, February 23, 1935, 9, 11; idem, "Velkhe rusishe yidn vil men shikn in Biro-Bidzhan?" *Forverts*, February 26, 1935, 3, 8; idem, "Tsu vos darf di sovet-regirung, az yidn zoln forn keyn Biro-Bidzhan?" *Forverts*, February 28, 1935, 6, 10.

64. Shimen Dimanshtein, *Di yidishe avtonome gegnt—a kind fun der oktober-revolyutsye* (Moscow: Emes, 1934), 41.

65. David Khait, "Storona Biorbidzhanskaia," *Bezbozhnik* 6 (1936): 8–9.

66. Perelman, *Birobidzhan*, 184.

67. See, for example, Inna Shtakser, *The Making of Jewish Revolutionaries in the Pale of Settlement: Community and Identity during the Russian Revolution and Its Immediate Aftermath, 1905–1907* (New York: Palgrave Macmillan, 2014), 43.

68. Natan Meir, "From Pork to *Kapores*: Transformation in Religious Practice among the Jews of Late Imperial Kiev," *Jewish Quarterly Review* 97.4 (2007): 628–30.

69. Rebecca E. Margolis, "A Tempest in Three Teapots: Yom Kippur Balls in London, New York, and Montreal," in *The Canadian Jewish Studies Reader*, eds. Richard Menkis and Norman Ravvin (Calgary, Canada: Red Deer Press, 2004), 141–63.

70. Barbara Kirshenblatt-Gimblett, "Recipes for Creating Community: The Jewish Charity Cookbook in America," *Jewish Folklore and Ethnology Review* 9.1–2 (1987): 8.

71. Brandon Schechter, "The State's Pot and the Soldier's Spoon: Rations (*Paëk*) in the Red Army," in *Hunger and War: Food Provisioning in the Soviet Union during World War II*, ed. Wendy Z. Goldman and Donald Filtzer (Bloomington IN: Indiana University Press, 2015), 110–11.

72. Elissa Bemporad, *Becoming Soviet Jews: The Bolshevik Experiment in Minsk* (Bloomington: Indiana University Press, 2013), 123.

73. See Ziva Galili, "The Soviet Experience of Zionism: Importing Soviet Political Culture to Palestine," *Journal of Israeli History* 24.1 (2005): 1–33.

74. See A. Deman, "Merderishe onfaln oyf yidishe kolonistn in Palestine," *Forverts*, April 14, 1920, 3.

75. Maurice Friedberg, "New Editions of Soviet Belles-Lettres: A Study in Politics and Palimpsests," *The American Slavic and East European Review* 13.1 (1954): 78.

76. Robert Weinberg, "Purge and Politics in the Periphery: Birobidzhan in 1937," *Slavic Review* 52.1 (1993): 27; Ekaterina Libinzon, "Birobidzhan: Moia liubov' i moia bol'," *Korni* 34 (2007): 26; Motl Sirota, "Vospominaniia: Zapiski aktera," *Lekhaim* 7 (2008): 37.

77. Alexander Ivanov, "V poiskakh novogo cheloveka na beregakh rek Biry i Bidzhana: Evreiskaia sektsiia Gosudarstvennogo muzeia etnografii v Leningrade (1937–1941)," in *Sovetskaia geniza: Novye arkhivnye razyskaniia po istorii evreev v SSSR*, vol. 1, ed. by Gennady Estraikh and Alexander Frenkel (Boston and Saint-Petersburg: Academic Studies Press, 2020), 236–237.

78. Druianov, *Evreskaia avtonomnaia oblast'*, 4–6.

Chapter 3

1. "Plans Made to Aid Jewish Settlers," *The New York Times*, December 18, 1935. 32; Ivanov, "Facing East," 369–388.

2. Joseph Rosen, "Experts Give Views on Biro-Bidjan: Its Development Feasible but a Gigantic Task," *Jewish Daily Bulletin*, November 9, 1934, 5 and 7.

3. James G. McDonald, *Advocate for the Doomed: The Diaries and Papers of James G. McDonald, 1932–1935* (Bloomington: Indiana University Press, 2007), 588.

4. David Brody, "American Jewry, the Refugees and Immigration Restrictions (1932–1942)," *Publications of the American Jewish Historical Society* 45. 4 (1956), 233.

5. "500 Jews Work, for ORT in Biro-Bidjan," *The Sentinel*, March 5, 1935, 33; "Plans Made to Aid Jewish Settlers."

6. Adolph Held, "Mayn ershter tog in Biro-Bidzhan," *Forverts*, September 8, 1936, 4–5.

7. Adolph Held, "Di 'lagernikes' vos boyen Biro-Bidzhan," *Forverts*, September 20, 1936, section 2, 1.

8. Lifshitz, *Khaloymes un virklekhkayt*, 74.

9. Adolph Held, "A geshprekh mit dem hoypt-firer fun Biro-Bidzhan," *Forverts*, September 10, 1936, 7–8.

10. Adolph Held, "Entfer oyf fragn vos m'shtelt vegn Biro-Bidzhan," *Forverts*, September 23, 1936, 6, 19; idem, "Vifl yidn kenen zikh bazetsn in Biro-Bidzhan?" *Forverts*, September 25, 1936, 8.

11. Alexander A. Troyanovsky, "Whole Soviet Union Helps to Build Biro-Bidzhan," *Jewish Advocate*, September 25, 1936, 11.

12. Alfred Segal, "Plain Talk: Pinya Kopman," *The American Israelite*, May 13, 1937, 1.

13. "Dr. Rozen shikt a briv tsum 'Forverts' vegn zayn rede iber Biro-Bidzhan," *Forverts*, December 22, 1936, 4; Gennadii V. Kostyrchenko, *Tainaia politika Stalina: Vlast´ i antisemitizm* (Moscow: Mezhdunarodnye otnosheniia, 2001), 119–121.

14. "O sovetskom, khoziaistvennom i kul'turnom stroitel'stve Evreiskoi avtonomnoi oblasti," *Birobidzhanskaia Pravda*, September 15, 1936, 1.

15. See, e.g., Yakov Milch, *Biro-Bidzhan: A naye epokhe in der yidisher geshikhte* (New York: ICOR, 1936), 41–42.

16. See, e.g., "Biro-Bidjan's Plan Lives, Says Envoy, Answering Rumor," *The American Israelite*, April 1, 1937, 1; "Liquidation of Birobidjan Plans Denied by Soviet," *The Southern Israelite*, April 2, 1937, 1.

17. See, in particular, Weinberg, "Purge and Politics in the Periphery," 13–27.

18. *Dal'nii Vostok Rossii v epokhu sovetskoi modernizatsii*, 180–190.

19. Ross King, "Blagoslovennoe: Korean Village on the Amur, 1971-1937," *The Review of Korean Studies* 4.2 (2001): 162–163; Michael Gelb, "An Early Soviet Ethnic Deportation: The Far-Eastern Koreans," *The Russian Review* 54.3 (1995): 389–341.

20. Aleksandr S. Suturin, *Delo kraevogo masshtaba* (Khabarovsk: Khabarovskoe knizhnoe izdatelstvo, 1991), 8.

21. Steven E. Merritt, The Great Purges in the Soviet Far East, 1937–1938. PhD dissertation (Riverside: University of California, 2000), 148.

22. Romanova and Korolev, "Iz istorii bor'by s antisemitizmom v EAO v 1935 g.," 6.

23. Yuri Slezkine, *The Jewish Century, New Edition* (Princeton: Princeton University Press, 2019), 274.

24. See Gennady Estraikh, "Pyrrhic Victories of Soviet Yiddish Language Planners," *East European Jewish Affairs* 23:2 (1993): 25–37.

25. Efim Melamed, "Kak byl unichtozhen venets evreiskoi kul'tury: evreiskie uchenye Kieva nakanune i vo vremia Bol'shogo terrora," in *Sovetskaia geniza: Novye arkhivnye razyskaniia po istorii evreev v SSSR*, vol. 1, ed. by Gennady Estraikh and Alexander Frenkel (Boston and Saint-Petersburg: Academic Studies Press, 2020), 139.

26. Esther Rosenthal-Shnaiderman, *Oyf vegn un umvegn: zikhroynes, gesheenishn, perzenlekhkaytn* (Tel Aviv: I. L. Peretz farlag, 1983), 82. For Rosenthal-Shnaiderman, see Iosif Brener, *Ester Rozental'-Shnaiderman: lichnyi arkhiv i birobidzhanskii sled* (Birobidzhan: Publishing house "Birobidzhan," 2022).

27. Matvei P. Khavkin, *Evreiskaia avtonomnaia oblast' k svoei pervoi godovshchine* (Moscow: Emes, 1935), 19–20.

28. Chaim Beider, "Khaim Holmshtok," *Sovetish heymland* 12 (1989): 126–127.

29. Esther Rosenthal-Shneiderman, *Birobidzhan fun der noent: zikhroynes, gesheenishn, perzenlekhkaytn* (Tel Aviv: H. Leyvik-Farlag, 1983), 188.

30. S. Iu. Gamalei, "Kadrovyi sostav natsional'nykh teatrov Dal'nego Vostoka v 1930-e gody (na primere evreiskogo teatra g. Birobidzhana," in *Voprosy razvitiia tvorcheskoi sredy Dal'nego Vostoka Rossii i Aziatsko-*

Tikhookeanskogo regiona, ed. by S. N. Skorinov (Khabarovsk: State Institute of Culture, 2018), 83.

31. Khavkin, *Evreiskaia avtonomnaia oblast' k svoei pervoi godovshchine*, 9.

32. Yehuda Slutsky, "Tribuna—a Soviet Jewish Russian Journal, 1927–1937," *Soviet Jewish Affairs* 12.2 (1982): 40.

33. Josef Baskin, *Saliuty i rasstrely: zapiski utselevshego* (Tel Aviv: Starlight, 1999), 71–74.

34. Weinberg, "Purge and Politics in the Periphery," 13–27.

35. Leonid Kuras, "SSSR—Manch'zhou-Go: 'evreiskii vopros' po obe storony granitsy (1934-1941 gg.)," *Izvestiia Irkutskogo gosudarstvennogo universiteta* 17 (2016): 90.

36. Gennadii Kostyrchenko, *V plenu u krasnogo faraona: politicheskie presledovaniya evreev v SSSR v poslednee stalinskoe desiatiletie* (Moscow: Mezhdunarodnye otnosheniia, 1994), 176.

37. *Literaturnyi Birobidzhan: proza, poeziia*, ed. Roman Shoikhet (Khabarovsk: Khabarovskoe knigoizdale'stvo, 1984), 5.

38. See Gennady Estraikh, *Evreiskaia literaturnaia zhisn' Moskvy, 1917–1991* (St Petersburg: The European University, 2015), 215–217, 241.

39. A. V., "Literaturnaia zhizn' Birobidzhana," *Literaturnaia gazeta*, September 26, 1939, 5.

40. Aleksandr A. Isaev, "Migratsionnye protsessy na Dal'nem Vostoke SSSR v 1930-e—pervoi polovine 1940-kh godov," *Gumanitarnye issledovaniia v Vostochnoi Sibiri i na Dal'nem Vostoke* 1 (2013): 40.

41. Gennadii Kostyrchenko, "Stalinskii perelom kontsa 1920-kh gg. v reshenii evreiskogo voprosa," *in 1929: "Velikii perelom" i ego posledstviia* (Moscow: Politicheskaia entsiklopediia, 2020), 144.

42. Irina Manoilenko, "Nezasluzhenno zabytyi," *Birobidzhaner Shtern*, May 16, 1918. https://www.gazetaeao.ru/nezasluzhenno-zabytyj-2/

Chapter 4

1. A. Landau, "Tev'e-molochnik—eksponent," *Izvestiia*, August 21, 1939, 3.

2. A. Gilman, *Vos darf visn an ibervanderer vegn der yidisher avtonomer gegnt* (Moscow: Emes, 1939), 23, 48–49.

3. *Istoriia Dal'nego Vostoka Rossii v epokhu sovetskoi modernizatsii: 1922—nachalo 1941gg.*, ed. by V. L Larin and L. I. Galiamov (Vladivostok: Dal'nauka, 2018), 114.

4. Lewis H. Siegelbaum and Leslie Page Moch, *Broad Is My Native Land: Repertoires and Regimes of Migration in Russia's Twentieth Century* (Ithaca, NY: Cornell University Press, 2015), 42.

5. See e.g., Viktoriia V. Romanova "Dal'nii Vostok i evropeiskie evrei v gody natsizma (1933-1945)," *Vestnik Tomskogo gosudarstvennogo universiteta* 65 (2020): 44.

6. Kostyrchenko, "Stalinskii perelom kontsa 1920-kh gg. v reshenii evreiskogo voprosa," 144.

7. Kotlerman, *In Search of Milk and Honey*, 163.

8. G. A. Tkacheva, "Dinamika chislennosti i sostava naseleniia Dal'nego Vostoka v 1941-1945 gg.," *Oikumena: Regional'nye issledovaniia* 1 (2007): 63; V. S. Gurevich, S. I. Kulikova and L. S. Paramonova, *Chasovye dalekoi voiny* (Birobidzhan: n.p., 2015), 5.

9. Kotlerman, *In Search of Milk and Honey*, 170.

10. *Birobidjan and the Jews in the Post-War World: A Series of Addresses to the U.S.A. of Prof. Mikhoels and Lt.-Col. Feffer of the U.S.S.R* (New York: Ambijan, 1943), 13, 19–20.

11. See Gennadii Kostyrchenko, "Proekt 1944 goda 'Evreiskaia respublika v Krymu': legendy i realii," in *Istoricheskie chteniia na Lubianke* (Moscow: Kuchkovo pole, 2008), 144–161.

12. *The Conference at Malta and Yalta, 1945. United States. Department of State* (Washington D.C.: US Government Printing Office, 1955), 924.

13. Kotlerman, *In Search of Milk and Honey*, 192.

14. David Vaiserman, *Birobidzhan: mechty i tragediia* (Khabarovsk: Knizhnoe izdatel'stvo, 1999), 113, 352, 353.

15. Robert Weinberg, "Jewish Revival in Birobidzhan in the Mirror of *Birobidzhanskaya zvezda*, 1946–49," *East European Jewish Affairs* 26.1 (1996): 40.

16. Vaiserman, *Birobidzhan*, 150, 158, 222.

17. Robert Weinberg, "Birobidzhan After the Second World War," *Jews in Eastern Europe* 3 (2002): 33–34.

18. "Afn moskver alshtotishn Sholem-Aleykhem-ovnt," *Eynikayt*, May 18, 1946, 2; "Der tsveyter Sholem-Aleykhem-ovnt in kolonen-zal," *Eynikayt*, May 25, 1942, 2.

19. For a detailed analysis of this journay, see Ber Boris Kotlerman, *Broken Heart / Broken Wholeness: The Post-Holocaust Plea for Jewish Reconstruction of the Soviet Yiddish Writer Der Nister* (Brighton, MA: Academic Studies Press, 2017).

20. Joseph Rabin, *Mir lebn* (Moscow: Emes, 1948), 68.

21. Mordechai Altshuler, *Soviet Jewry on the Eve of the Holocaust: A Social and Demographic Profile* (Jerusalem: Hebrew University and Yad Vashem, 1998), 190.

22. Elena S. Genina, "Evreiskie obshchiny Khabarovskogo kraia v seredine 1940-kh—nachale 1950-kh gg," *Vestnik Kemerovskogo gosudarstvennogo universiteta* 3 (2012): 47–51; Ber Kotlerman, "If There Had Been No Synagogue There, They Would Have Had to Invent It: The Case of the Birobidzhan 'Religious Community of the Judaic creed' on the Threshold of Perestroika," *East European Jewish Affairs* 42.2 (2012): 89.

23. See Gennady Estraikh, *Yiddish in the Cold War* (Oxford: Legenda, 2008), 41–42.

24. Weinberg, "Birobidzhan After the Second World War," 35.

25. Gennadii Kostyrchenko, *Gosudarstvennyi antisemitizm v SSSR ot nachala do kul'minatsii, 1938–1953* (Moscow: Mezhdunarodnyi fond "Demokratiia"/Materik, 2005), 6–7.

26. Mikhail Romm, "The Question of the National Question, or A Rally for a Genuinely Russian Cinema," in *Soviet Jews in World War II: Fighting, Witnessing, Remembering*, ed. by Harriet Murav and Gennady Estraikh (Boston: Academic Studies Press, 2014), 219.

27. Kotlerman, *In Search of Milk and Honey*, 218.

28. "Dedov—Stalinu ob ideologicheskoi rabote v Evreiskoi avtonomnoi oblasti," June 26, 1949. Fond Aleksandra N. Iakovleva. https://www.alexanderyakovlev.org/fond/issues-doc/1016222.

29. "Jewish Autonomous Oblast," Freedom of Information Act Electronic Reading Room. https://www.cia.gov/readingroom. CIA-RDP8000810A004100660005–9.

30. Gennady Estraikh, "Birobidzhan in Khrushchev's Thaw: The Soviet and the Western Outlook," *Journal of Modern Jewish Studies* 18.1 (2019): 60.

31. D. V. Korolev, "Kampaniia po bor'be s 'burzhuaznym natsionalizmom' v srede birobidzhanskikh pisatelei v 1948 g.," in *Evrei v Sibiri i na Dal'nem Vostoke: istoriia i sovremennost'*, ed. Iakov M. Kofman, Krasnoiarsk: Kranoiarskii pisatel, 2007, 143–155; Kotlerman, *In Search of Milk and Honey*, 224, 232.

32. Yitshok Katsnelson, "Di yidishe kultur-manifestatsye in Moskve," *Folks-Shtime*, May 29, 1956, 3. For Miller's rehabilitation, see also Brener, *Ester Rozental'-Shnaiderman*, 84.

Notes

Chaper 5

1. *American Workers Look at the Soviet Union: Impressions of the American Trade Union Delegation that Visited the Soviet Union in June and July 1951* (Moscow: Foreign Languages Publishing House, 1952), 86.

2. Benjamin Pinkus, *The Soviet Government and the Jews, 1948–1967: A Documented Study* (Cambridge, UK, and New York: Cambridge University Press, 1984), 351.

3. Edward Crankshaw, "Russia Abolishes Jewish Province," *The Observer*, May 20, 1951, 3.

4. Friedberg, "New Editions of Soviet Belles-Lettres," 78.

5. "Birobidzhan Help Called Diverted," *The New York Times*, September 23, 1954, 5.

6. Leonid Leshchinskii, *Mig zhizni (memuary)*. http://samlib.ru/l/leshinskij_leonid_abramowich/doc116.shtml.

7. Radik Sandik, *V neoplatnom dolgu; vospominaniia* (Jerusalem: Filobiblon, 2019), 59.

8. Yurii Kapkov, *Oskolki pamiati* (St Petersburg: n.p., 2004), 305.

9. See Gennady Estraikh, "The Rise of Ilya Yegudin: An Exemplary Jew in Soviet Agriculture," *East European Jewish Affairs* (forthcoming).

10. See, e.g., Andrei Prishvin, "Shchedraia zemlia," *Pravda*, March 25, 1956, 3.

11. "Rech' tovarishcha N. S. Khrushcheva," *Pravda*, January 22, 1956, 2.

12. "Memorandum. From Paris Office to Foreign Affairs Department. May 17, 1961," Records of the American Jewish Committee, Paris Office. YIVO Archives. RG347.7.41, box 50, file 475.

13. See Gerald Tulchinsky, "Family Quarrel: Joe Salsberg, the 'Jewish' Question, and Canadian Communism," *Labour/Le Travail* 56 (2005), 149–173; Estraikh, *Yiddish in the Cold War*, 25–26.

14. "Letter from J. Edgar Hoover to Allen W. Dulles," Freedom of Information Act Electronic Reading Room. https://www.cia.gov/readingroom. CIA-RDP80B01676R001000010005–7.

15. Stephen H. Norwood, *Antisemitism and the American Left* (New York: Cambridge University Press, 2013), 185.

16. In fact, Jews did work in building or metallurgy—see, e.g., Viacheslav Konstantinov, *Evreiskoe naselenie byvshego SSSR v XX veke* (Jerusalem: n.p., 2007), 220.

17. Pinkus, *The Soviet Government and the Jews*, 62.

18. Nahum Goldman, "Khrushchev and the Soviet Jews," *New York Herald Tribune*, May 7, 1958, 18.

19. NORTHERN (N): Soviet Union (NS). Community of Jews at Birobidjan in Soviet Union (FO371–135342). Great Britain. Foreign Office. Political Departments (Abingdon, England: Taylor & Francis; London: Foreign Office 9999).

20. Pinkus, *The Soviet Government and the Jews*, 382.

21. The Database *Cold War in Eastern Europe* (Taylor & Francis). Files from the Political Departments of the U.K. Foreign Office. "Extract from Summary Record of Conversation between the Prime Minister [Harold Macmillan] and Mr. Khrushchev at Dinner on February 23 [1959]," cwee. fo371.152020.001pdf.

22. Harry Schwartz, "Moscow Depicts Birobidzhan Life," *The New York Times*, August 31, 1958, 23.

23. See, in particular, Judd L. Teller, "Exit of Jews to Siberia Hinted," *The Chriatian Science Monitor*, January 5, 1959, 4; Marianne Rachel Sanua, *Let Us Prove Strong: The American Jewish Committee* (Hanover, NH, 2007), 120.

24. Joseph Heller, *The United States, the Soviet Union and the Arab-Israeli conflict, 1948–67: Superpower Rivalry* (Manchester: Manchester University Press, 2010), 102.

25. See, e.g., Judd L. Teller, "Exit of Jews to the Siberia Hinted," *The Christian Science Monitor*, January 5, 1959, 4; Irving Spiegel, "Jews' Resettling by Soviet Is Seen: U.S. Group Says Moscow May Develop Birobidzhan Under 7-Year Plan," *The New York Times*, January 11, 1959, 2.

26. See, e.g., Samson Madievski and Françoize Cordes, "1953: La déportation des juifs soviétiques était-elle programmée?" *Cahiers du Monde russe* 41.4 (2000): 561–568; Gennadii V. Kostyrchenko, "Deportatsiia— mistifikatsiia: proshchanie s mifom stalinskoi epokhi," *Otechestvennaia istoriia* 1 (2003): 92–113; Victor H. Winston, "Reflections on the Anticipated Mass Deportation of Soviet Jews," *Post-Soviet Affairs* 31.6 (2015): 471–490.

27. Murray Seeger, "Exodus to the Wastelands," *The Guardian*, November 30, 1972, 17.

28. Heller, *The United States, the Soviet Union and the Arab-Israeli Conflict*, 41.

29. A. Wiseman and O. Pick, "Soviet Jews under Khrushchev," *Commentary* 27.2 (1959): 127–132.

30. JDC Archive, document NY AR2132 00733.

31. Pietro A. Shakarian, An Armenian Reformer in Khrushchev's Kremlin: Anastas Mikoyan and the Politics of Difference in the USSR, 1953–1964.

PhD dissertation (The Ohio State University, 2021), 30. See also Estraikh, "Birobidzhan in Khrushchev's Thaw," 65–66.

32. "Mikoyan Bars Jews Visitors," *Jewish Advocate*, January 15, 1959, 1; "Mikoyan Denies Planned Exile of Jews to Siberia," *The American Israelite*, January 22, 1959, 1.

33. Except from memo by Eugene Henesi to Ralph Friedman, January 2, 1959. www.ajcarchives/AJC_DATA/Files/516.PDF.

34. "Mikoyan on Biro-Bidjan," *The Jewish Chronicle*, January 23, 1959, 13.

35. "Soviet Attitudes," *The Jewish Chronicle*, January 23, 1959, 16.

36. We learn this from the blurb on the back cover of a collection of Vergelis's propaganda speeches and interviews: *A Traveller's Encounters: Articles, Speeches, travel Notes, Interviews and Letters of a Jewish Poet* (Moscow: Novosti Press Agency, 1988).

37. Max Frankel, "Jewish Birobidzhan Is Found Quiet Corner in Brisk Siberia," *The New York Times*, May 1, 1959, 1.

38. Shmuel L. Shneiderman, "Tsvey yidn fun Biro-Bidzhan dertseyln zeyere iberlebungen," *Forverts*, December 10, 1959, 2.

39. Svetlana N. Mishchuk, "Retrospektivnyi analiz migratsionnykh protsessov v Evreiskoi avtonomnoi oblasti," *Regional'nye problemy* 18.3 (2015): 75.

40. Alice Andrews, "Spatial Patterns of Higher Education in the Soviet Union," *Soviet Geography* 7 (1978): 455.

41. Dominik Horodyński, *Syberia inaczej* (Warsaw: Wydawnictwo Ministerwa Obrony Narodowej, 1959), 70.

42. Ber Boris Kotlerman, "Ostanovi ruku tvoiu!: Pis'ma na ivrite iz Birobidzhana, god 1958-oi," in *Sovetskaia geniza: novye arkhivnye razyskaniia po istorii evreev v SSSR*, ed. by Gennady Estraikh, and Alexander Frenkel (St Petersburg and Boston: Academic Studies Press, 2020), 368, 393–394.

43. The Database *Cold War in Eastern Europe* (Taylor & Francis). Files from the Political Departments of the U.K. Foreign Office. Northern (N): Soviet Union (NS). Weekly Round-Up of Miscellaneous News and Gossip from HM Embassy, 1961. cwee.fo371/159537/001.

44. A. Vinokur, "Ugasanie drevnei very," *Nauka i religiia* 1 (1967): 41–43.

45. Elehie Skoczylas, *The Realities of Soviet Anti-Semitism* (Philadelphia: University of Pennsylvania, Foreign Policy Research Institute, 1965), 12.

46. Konstantinov, *Evreiskoe naselenie byvshego SSSR v XX veke*, 20.

Chapter 6

1. Harrison E. Salisbury, "Birobidzhan Jews Drop Yiddish, Prefer Russian, Visitor Is Told," *The New York Times*, June 22, 1954, 6.

2. Olga P. Zhuravleva, "Periodicheskaia pechat' Evreiskoi avtonomnoi oblasti (1928–1960gg.)," in *Birobidzhanskii proekt: opyt mezhnatsional'nogo vzaimodeistviia*, eds. By V. S. Gurevich *et al.* (Birobidzhan: The JAR's Government, 2008), 89.

3. Pinkus, *The Soviet Government and the Jews*, 379.

4. Salisbury, "Birobidzhan Jews Drop Yiddish."

5. "The Visit to Khabarovsk and Birobidzhan of Israeli Ambassador to Moscow Yosef Avidar and His Wife, Yemima Tchernovitz (1956): Excerpt from Yemima's Diary," introduced and annotated by Yaacov Ro'i, in *Mizrekh: Jewish Studies in the Far East*, ed. by Ber Boris Kotlerman (Frankfurt am Main, 2009), 154.

6. Artur Patek, "The Jewish Autonomous Oblast in the USSR in the Documents of the British Foreign Office (1952–1958)," *Scripta Judaica Cracoviensia* 17 (2019): 116.

7. Ber Kotlerman, "Toska vliublennogo, govoriashchego o svoei vozliublennoi," *Narod knigi v mire knig* 128 (1928): 1–6.

8. "New Light on Biro-Bidjan," *Jewish Advocate*, December 1, 1955, A2; "More Red Propaganda," *Jewish Advocate*, December 15, 1955, A2; "In a novine—oyfgedekt a farloymdung vegn Biro-Bidzhan," *Morgn-Frayhayt*, January 1, 1956, 5.

9. Zhuravleva, "Periodicheskaia pechat" Evreiskoi avtonomnoi oblasti', 90.

10. See, e.g., Sloves, *In un arum*, 145.

11. Frankel, "Jewish Birobidzhan Is Found Quiet Corner in Brisk Siberia"; idem, "Siberia's New Look," *Los Angeles Times*, May 1, 1959, 1.

12. See, e.g., Solomon Rabinovich, "Vos dertseylt 'Biro-Bidzhaner shtern'?" *Morgn-Frayhayt*, January 3, 1957, 5; idem, "Tipn fun yidn in Biro-Bidzhan," *Morgn-Frayhayt*, January 15, 1957, 5.

13. "Paul Novic, David Matis, and Abraham Bick," Freedom of Information Act Electronic Reading Room. https://www.cia.gov/readingroom. CIA-RDP91–00965R000500120021–0.

14. Solomon Rabinovich, *Jews in the Soviet Union* (Moscow: Novosti Press Agency Publishing House, 1965), 28–29.

15. See Gennady Estraikh, "Paul Novick, a Standard-Bearer of Yiddish Communism," in *A Vanished Ideology: Essays on the Jewish Communist*

Movement in the English-Speaking World in the Twentieth Century, ed. by Matthew B. Hoffman and Henry F. Srebrnik (Albany: State University of New York Press, 2016), 93.

16. Sid Resnik, "Birobidjan, Soviet Jews and Anti-Semitism," in *The Soviet Jewish Situation: A Progressive View* (New York: Jewish Currents, 1980), 15.

17. Albert Axelbank, "A 'Jewish National State?'" *Present Tense: The Magazine of World Jewish Affairs* 4.1 (1976): 20.

18. Tevye Gen, "In Birobidzhan," in his *A veg in der vayt* (Moscow: Sovetskii pisatel', 1977), 363–404.

19. "Pasport Birobidzhanskogo narodnogo teatra Khabarovskogo kraia," Russian State Archive of Literature and Art, f. 970 op. 22 ed. khr. 1596.

20. Iosef S. Brener, *Lekhaim, Birobidzhan!* (Krasnoiarsk: Krasnoiarskii pisatel', 2007), 177–178.

21. Yurii Sherling, *Odinochestvo dlinoiu v zhisn'* (Moscow: Paralleli, 2004), 185.

22. Aron Vergelis, "Ekzotishe tayge," *Birobidzhaner shtern*, September 11, 1960, 4.

23. Viacheslav Kostikov, *The People and Land of Birobidzhan: The Jewish Autonomous Regio*n (Moscow: Novosti Press Agency, 1979), 23, 25.

24. Leonid Shkolnik, "Birobidzhan: Jewish Autonomy—To Be or not to Be?" *Jewish Quarterly* 37.4 (1990): 23.

25. Horodyński, *Syberia inaczej*, 71.

26. Elena Sarashevskaia, "Idish—moia strast," *Birobidzhaner Shtern*, October 5, 2016. https://www.gazetaeao.ru/idish-moya-strast/

27. Gennady Estraikh and Iosef S. Brener, "'Birobidzhanskoe pokolenie': stroitel'stvo mestechka na Dal'nem Vostoke," *Judaic-Slavic Journal* 1 (2021): 214.

28. Axelbank, "A 'Jewish National State?'" 20.

29. Mark Tolts, "Mass Aliyah and Jewish Emigration from Russia: Dynamics and Factors," *East European Jewish Affairs* 33.2, (2003): 71–96.

30. *Sionizm—otravlennoe oruzhie imperializma*, ed. by O. V. Vadeev (Moscow: Politizdat, 1970), 225.

31. Mark Tolts, "The Post-Soviet Jewish Population in Russia and the World," *Jews in Russia and Eastern Europe* 1 (2004): 50–51.

32. Shaun Walker, "Revival of a Soviet Zion: Birobidzhan celebrates its Jewish heritage," *The Guardian*, September 17, 2017. https://www.theguardian.

com/world/2017/sep/27/revival-of-a-soviet-zion-birobidzhan-celebrates-
its-jewish-heritage.

Chapter 7

1. Matvei D. Pinshchuk, "'Respubliki ne budet: Evreiskaia AO i ee put'
   k samostoiatel'nosti v 1990-1991 gg.," in *Levye ideologii, dvizheniia i
   organizatsii v istorii*, ed. by A. K. Sorokin (Moscow: ROSSPEN, 2019),
   317–320.

2. Leonid Bliakher, "Kto takie 'evreitsy,' ili Opyt kulturnogo sinteza na
   Amure," *Idei i idealy* (2018): 172–190.

3. Alina Ivanova and Andrei Kovalevskii, "Arkhitekturnyi landshaft
   Evreiskoi avtonomnoi oblasti," *Proekt Baikal* 65 (2020): 104–111.

4. S. I. (Shelley) Salamensky, "'Jewface' and 'Jewfaçade' in Poland, Spain,
   and Birobidzhan," in *The Routledge Handbook to Contemporary Jewish
   Cultures*, edited by Nadia Valman and Laurence Roth (Abingdon and
   New York: Routledge, 2015), 220. The author treats Aleichem as the
   writer's surname, though it is part of his pseudonym, meaning "peace to
   you."

5. Ibid.

SELECTED BIBLIOGRAPHY

Bergelson, David. *The Jewish Autonomous Region* (Moscow: Foreign Languages Publishing House, 1939).

Birobidjan and the Jews in the Post-War World: A Series of Addresses to the U.S.A. of Prof. Mikhoels and Lt.-Col. Feffer of the U.S.S.R (New York: Ambijan, 1943).

Estraikh, Gennady. "Birobidzhan in Khrushchev's Thaw: The Soviet and the Western Outlook," *Journal of Modern Jewish Studies* 18.1 (2019): 56–74.

Estraikh, Gennady. "Literary Images of the 'Birobidzhan Generation'," *Slavic Almanac* 11.1 (2005): 78–95.

Estraikh, Gennady. "Yiddish Language Conference Aborted," *East European Jewish Affairs* 25.2 (1995): 91–96.

Frankel, Max. "Jewish Birobidzhan Is Found Quiet Corner in Brisk Siberia," *The New York Times*, May 1, 1959, 1.

Gelb, Michael. "An Early Soviet Ethnic Deportation: The Far-Eastern Koreans," *The Russian Review* 54.3 (1995): 389–341.

Goldberg, Ben Zion. *The Jewish Problem in the Soviet Union: Analysis and Solution* (New York: Crown Publishers, 1961).

Gurevitz, Baruch. "The Liquidation of the Last Independent Party in the Soviet Union," *Canadian Slavonic Papers* 18.2 (1976): 178–186.

Lord Marley, *Biro Bidjan as I Saw It* (New York: ICOR, 1935).

Kagedan, Allan L. "American Jews and the Soviet Experiment: The Agro-Joint Project, 1924–1937," Jewish Social Studies, 42.2 (1981): 153–164.

Kagedan, Allan L. *Soviet Zion: The Quest for a Russian Homeland* (New York: Palgrave Macmillan, 1994).

Kotlerman, Ber Boris. "If There Had Been No Synagogue There, They Would Have Had to Invent It: The Case of the Birobidzhan Religious Community of the Judaic Creed on the Threshold of Perestroika," *East European Jewish Affairs* 42.2 (2012): 87–97.

Kotlerman, Ber Boris. *In Search of Milk and Honey: The Theater of 'Soviet Jewish Statehood' (1934–49)* (Bloomington: Slavica Publishers, 2009).

Kotlerman, Ber Boris. "The Image of Birobidzhan in Soviet Yiddish Belles Letters," *Jews in Eastern Europe* (2002): 47–78.

Kotlerman, Ber Boris. "'Why I am in favour of Birobidzhan': Bergelson's Fateful Decision," in *David Bergelson: From Modernism to Socialist Realism*, ed. by Joseph Sherman and Gennady Estraikh (Oxford: Legenda, 2007), 222–235.

Selected Bibliography

Patek, Artur. "The Jewish Autonomous Oblast in the USSR in the Documents of the British Foreign Office (1952–1958)," *Scripta Judaica Cracoviensia* 17 (2019): 105–120.

Salisbury, Harrison E. "Birobidzhan Jews Drop Yiddish, Prefer Russian, Visitor Is Told," *The New York Times*, June 22, 1954, 6.

Schwartz, Harry. "Moscow Depicts Birobidzhan Life," *The New York Times*, August 31, 1958, 23.

Srebrnik, Henry F. *Dreams of Nationhood: American Jewish Communists and the Soviet Birobidzhan Project, 1924–1951* (Boston: Academic Studies Press, 2010).

"The Visit to Khabarovsk and Birobidzhan of Israeli Ambassador to Moscow Yosef Avidar and His Wife, Yemima Tchernovitz (1956): Excerpt from Yemima's Diary," introduced and annotated by Yaacov Ro'i, in *Mizrekh: Jewish Studies in the Far East*, ed. by Ber Boris Kotlerman (Frankfurt am Main: Peter Lang, 2009), 141–170.

Weinberg, Robert. "Birobidzhan After the Second World War," *Jews in Eastern Europe* 3 (2002): 31–46.

Weinberg, Robert. "Jewish Revival in Birobidzhan in the Mirror of *Birobidzhanskaya zvezda*, 1946–49," *East European Jewish Affairs* 26.1 (1996): 35–53.

Weinberg, Robert. "Purge and Politics in the Periphery: Birobidzhan in 1937," *Slavic Review* 52.1 (1993): 13–27.

Weinberg, Robert. *Stalin's Forgotten Zion: Birobidzhan and the Making of a Soviet Jewish Homeland: An Illustrated History, 1928–1996* (Berkeley: University of California Press, 1998).

INDEX

Index

Index